W9-BUT-416

Ten years ago Norman Vincent Peale wrote THE POWER OF POSITIVE THINKING, which introduced new techniques in solving personal problems . . . and brought hope and strength to millions of people.

Today, people everywhere face problems vastly greater than those of a decade ago: personal problems, national problems, international problems. In this new book

THE TOUGH-MINDED OPTIMIST

Dr. Peale adds a new dimension, a new depth of understanding and new ways to surmount the stumbling blocks to our happiness and well-being. He offers sound, practical, imaginative means to turn daily defeats into ultimate victories.

To the "Tough-Minded Optimist" the problems that might be *stumbling blocks,* become, instead, *building blocks* to personal progress, to the serenity of mind and spirit so necessary to vital living.

ABOUT THE AUTHOR

Pastor of the Marble Collegiate Church in New York City, Dr. Norman Vincent Peale is famous for his best sellers, *A Guide to Confident Living, The Power of Positive Thinking, Stay Alive All Your Life, The Amazing Results of Positive Thinking*, and many more. He is in constant demand as a popular public speaker and as a leader in civic affairs. He also writes a syndicated newspaper column and is Editor of Guideposts Magazine. He is President of the American Foundation for Religion and Psychiatry and Chairman of the Foundation for Christian Living.

THE
TOUGH-MINDED
OPTIMIST

BOOKS BY NORMAN VINCENT PEALE

The Amazing Results of Positive Thinking
Stay Alive All Your Life
Inspiring Messages for Daily Living
The Power of Positive Thinking
A Guide to Confident Living
Not Death At All
You Can Win
The Art of Living

(With Dr. Smiley Blanton)
The Art of Real Happiness
Faith Is the Answer

THE
TOUGH-MINDED
OPTIMIST

by

NORMAN
VINCENT
PEALE

Prentice-Hall, Inc.
Englewood Cliffs, N.J.

BJ
1581.2
.P4

170
P358

Copyright, 1961, by Prentice-Hall, Inc., Englewood Cliffs, N.J.
All rights reserved, including the right to reproduce this
book, or any portions thereof, in any form, except for the
inclusion of brief quotations in a review. Library of Congress
Catalog Number 61–16714.

*Copyright under International and Pan-American Copyright
Conventions.*

Printed in the United States of America

92558-T

59857

*To the members and friends of Marble Collegiate
Church, New York City, whose loyal friendship has meant
more to me than I can ever express, this book is
affectionately dedicated.*

NORMAN VINCENT PEALE

A WORD TO THE READER

If you want to live in this tough world and still have some real faith and optimism this book is for you.

When you have what it takes to deal creatively with the harsh facts of human existence and still keep on believing in good outcomes, you are a tough-minded optimist. And in our book that is a high-quality designation of anyone.

That word *tough* is really quite a word. And it doesn't mean swaggering, sneering or hard-boiled à la hoodlum. Take a look at Webster's definition; it's a masterpiece:

> *Tough:* Having the quality of being strong or firm in texture, but flexible and not brittle; yielding to force without breaking; capable of resisting great strain without coming apart.

To have resiliency under the application of force and not break apart, to have good substantial texture of personality: *that* is to be tough in its upper-level meaning.

Since to get this way depends for the most part on how you think, whether with weakness or strength, timorousness or fearlessness, hesitancy or forthrightness; add toughness to your mental attitude and you've got an admixture that is something special, very special. When you are tough-minded you can endure strain and not break apart in your thoughts. And that's important too, for if you break in your thoughts you will indeed come apart.

But to endure and merely hold the line is not enough. The psychiatrist who asserted that "the chief duty of man is to endure life" told only half the story, and the poorer half, at that. To attack, to overcome, to achieve victory, to go forward is the better half of life's story. And so to the formula "tough-minded" we add the upbeat word *optimist*. Here again is a word that has taken on an inadequate connotation, for it is not a description of the super-cheery, the ultra-bright or the fortuitous. It is rather to see the worst in complete realism, but still to believe in the best. Again, Webster:

> *Optimism:* The doctrine that the goods of life overbalance the pain and evil of it, that life is preponderantly good. The inclination to put the most favorable construction upon actions and happenings, minimize adverse aspects, conditions and possibilities, or anticipate the best possible outcome; a cheerful and hopeful temperament.

A "Tough-Minded Optimist" then is one who doesn't break apart in his thoughts whatever the stress and who continues hopefully and cheerfully to expect the good no matter what the apparent situation. Perhaps Mrs. Alan Shepard, wife of America's first Astronaut, expressed the philosophy quite well in describing her attitude as her husband made his leap into space: "I believe in the power of good and of God. I felt goodness all around me and I knew Alan was in his right place and that he was in the hands of God. I slept well . . ."

Still another illustration of the tough-minded optimist is given by Alan Moorehead in his fascinating book on Africa *The White Nile*. He describes David Livingstone, famous explorer and missionary, in an unforgettable characterization. "He had that quality which the Arabs describe as *baraka*. In the most improbable circumstances he had the power of enhancing life and making it appear better than it was before. His mere presence seems to have conferred a blessing on everyone who met him."

Call the roll of life's troubles—sickness, pain, danger, fear, hatred, prejudice, war, and on and on. There's one type of person who has what it takes, who by God's help is equal to any or all of it: THE TOUGH-MINDED OPTIMIST.

NORMAN VINCENT PEALE

CONTENTS

ONE

HAVE WHAT IT TAKES
TO TAKE IT

Let's face it—to live in this particular world you've just got to be strong. Without strength you'll be crushed or at least crumpled. If this seems a bit on the grim side, call the roll of all the things that happen to people—pain, sickness, frustration, accident, disappointment, failure, double-dealing, to name only a few.

One thing every one must learn is how to have what it takes to take it. If you haven't yet had to take it you will, eventually. Something will hit you sometime, and unless you develop some real inner resistance it will rock you. So let's take a look at the sources of the strength you and I need.

The first thing is to develop some real good inner toughness. Inner toughness, tough-mindedness is a quality of top priority. Actually there are two kinds of people in this world, the tender-minded and the tough-minded. The tender-minded cannot take it. Criticism just cuts them to the quick. It hurts and wounds them terribly. Problems and obstacles appall them. Adversity and opposition overwhelm them. The poor, miserable tender-minded!

But there are also the tough-minded. They do not like criticism any better than anyone else. But they know how to receive and handle it. They carefully extract from criticism all the know-how it contains and simply blow the chaff away.

Problems and obstacles only serve to challenge them and they are completely unabashed by adversity and opposition. They are quite some people, the impressive and inspiring tough-minded. They have grown strong on the inside. They have what it takes.

Look deeply into yourself and down in your personality you will come upon the toughness the Creator put into you when He created you. He very well knew what you would be up against in this life and made you equal to it, to all of it. In fact, you are tougher than you think. If you have not exercised your spiritual "muscles," naturally, without use, they grow soft like any muscle. As you re-activate your basic toughness through use, it will develop and grow stronger.

I've been told that Frank Leahy, one time coach at Notre Dame and creator of some stellar football teams, wrote a legend in gigantic letters on the locker room wall. It was the last thing the players saw as they trotted out to the football field—"When the going gets tough, let the tough get going." Write that thought in large letters in your consciousness, and the tough in you will indeed get going and keep on going when circumstances become difficult.

It could be that the world was made as it is, full of problems and difficulty, to bring out this tough quality in human beings. What is almighty God attempting to do with us? There must be some purpose, else it's a huge, grim joke, and not so funny at that. I wonder if His purpose isn't to make strong, controlled people, who can handle life on earth so well that they deserve eternal life. If this isn't it, why, then, did He create us in His own image? Surely that was done in the expectation that ultimately we might be like Him. And in addition to goodness and love that means being strong, real strong.

One way to cultivate your potential inner tough-resistant quality is simply to hold a firm mental picture of yourself as possessing it. Practice "seeing" yourself, not as weak, wishy-washy and vascillating, but as strong, controlled, purposeful. You tend to become just what you picture yourself as being.

To help visualize yourself in terms of this strong mental pattern, I suggest the daily use of the following affirmation: "God made me strong. I see myself as I really am—strong. With God's help I am not weak; I am strong. I have what it takes. Thank you God for my strength."

Keep saying this, believing this. Keep practicing it too and in due course your conscious mind will accept your affirmation as fact. Strength becoming firmly established in your subconscious will become your determinative personality characteristic. For you are what your subconscious mind really believes that you are.

A plain sort of middle-aged woman came for a consultation, her husband remained in the outer office, for she wanted to talk with me alone.

"Our seventeen-year-old son has been arrested in an automobile theft," she explained, "and he's in other trouble, too. I know all the facts, but Dad doesn't as yet. I've been afraid for him to know. You see, he can't take things like this as well as I can, so I've got to handle it. I want you to help me buck my husband up so this blow won't crush him."

I couldn't help admiring this strong woman. Maybe she had over-pampered her husband, making him, in effect, into an older child to satisfy, perhaps, some deep mother instinct. But she surely had what it takes to face a bitterly difficult family problem. Admiringly I asked, "Where did you get this strength? You're really quite a person."

"Well," she replied, "we are poor people. We have had to struggle and scrimp. It seems everything has always come the hard way. We have gotten along, but never had much, and I

was raised in the same kind of home as a girl." Her simple recital, with not a vestige of complaint or bitterness, impressed
me. She continued, "I soon saw that Jack (her husband) was
an awfully nice fellow, but without much ability or ambition.
So I had to take charge of the family. I had to be strong and
I was made strong by God's help. I just made up my mind to
be strong, and that's all there is to it."

Well, that may be all there is to it, but, believe me, that is
plenty. She was truly a tough-minded optimist. Get this clear:
real strength is in you whether you know it or not. Moreover,
you have within you all the strength you will ever need to
handle anything you will ever have to face.

When this fundamental concept of inherent strength is
firmly established in your thought pattern, you will be able to
stand up to anything and not crack under it, no matter how
critical or difficult. And when you know deep in your mind
that you do have what it takes, you won't be so nervous or
tense or fearful about difficult matters. You will have a calm
and confident sense of capacity with much less doubt of your
ability to meet situations.

I have seen this strength develop in some defeated people,
so I know what can be done through our method of building
up strength. Take this difficult case for example.

I entered the coffee shop of a big city hotel early one morning. Glancing about I saw a man sitting alone at a table in
the corner and noted that his head was bowed in his hands,
elbows resting on the table. He gave the impression of anxiety
and weariness, and the thought crossed my mind that he might
be praying. Then I got busy with my breakfast and became
absorbed in the morning newspaper and gave no further
thought to this individual.

Presently I heard my name spoken and looking up, saw this
same man standing before me with a look of surprise, "I'll be
——!" he said.

"How come?" I asked. "Why are you requesting to be damned?"

Dropping into a chair alongside me he said, "Maybe prayers do get answered. I'm having a real tough time of it and I was sitting over there gulping down some breakfast and feeling like telling everyone and everything to go to h———. Then the thought of praying popped into my mind. I do pray, you know, sometimes. So I said, 'God, please help me. Please send me some help and do it quickly.' I don't know what brought you here, but I know one thing. You're the answer to a maiden's prayer."

"Well, let's get this straight," I replied, "I definitely believe in God's guidance and if God wants to use me to help you, I shall indeed be glad. But please don't get the idea I'm any wonder worker." I agreed to meet him later that day to explore his problem and see what we might do to help.

"I can't take all they throw at me," he stormed, when we met for an hour at five o'clock that afternoon. "It's too much. I feel like I'm going to explode, in fact, blow up. I just can't stand the gaff—that's all. I'm busting up under this strain. It isn't worth it; it just isn't worth it." He flopped into a chair, threw the telephone directory plunk against the wall, and again vehemently consigned everything to the hot place below.

"Go on," I said. "Give me the whole works and I'll send out for some more telephone directories to hurl at that wall if you like."

He grinned and calmed down some, but it was obvious that the poor man was highly conflicted and nervous. And as it came out, he was full of guilt and frustration. "You see," he continued, "I have had this terrific ambition all my life—this urge to go places, to be the top guy. Where did it get me? Sure, I've made money, but in your religious terminology, 'I've lost my soul.' Yeah, that's it. I've lost my soul. That's it exactly.

"I was a poor boy from the other side of the tracks. I used to watch those stuffed shirt bankers, lawyers and merchants driving their big cars and hanging around the country club. I hated 'em—and believe it or not, I still hate 'em . . . the lousy jerks. But even so, I wanted to join 'em, to have what they had . . . cars, country clubs and all that stuff. And I actually wanted to be a big shot like them . . . a lousy, phony, big shot, just like them. And so I got to doing all the putrid things some of them do, and believe me, I mean putrid. And I am fed up. I'm sick of the whole d——— racket."

What a story he poured out, and poured is the word. I put my feet up on the window sill and listened, and I heard the low down on suburbia in a style that went reams beyond the descriptive ability of our nasty novelists. They simply were not in it with this explosively disgusted denizen of big shotism.

"Boy, you should have been a writer. You could wield a wicked pen, and I don't mean maybe."

Unconsciously I was adopting his own racy style. That the man had something beyond the annoyance that was plaguing him was obvious. Actually his soul was showing. And that is always impressive.

When you are dealing with a tough, hard-fisted guy, you don't hand him out any soft, namby-pamby answers. You are up against an honesty and forthrightness that must be equalled in kind. I could have advised him to see a counselor. Indeed, he could have used some therapy, and later on I did bring this to him. But at the moment he needed the direct application of a healing force that was uncomplicated, one that had a cutting edge powerful enough to hack through the mass of rotten stuff with which he was filled. So, in his own language I gave him the "spiritual works."

Further evidence that God's guidance was working in this case seemed a coincidence. Suddenly the sound of hymns played by carillon bells came through the open window and as darkness fell a gigantic illuminated cross stood out against the night sky.

"Do you know anything about theology?" I asked my friend.

"Theology?" he repeated in bewilderment.

I pointed to the cross, high atop an office-building-church, twenty-five stories above the street. "That is at the center of theology. On it, once, the Savior died to show that God cares about us and loves us. I don't pretend to understand what happens, but I have found it to be a fact that, when people like you and me look to that cross and the Man who died on it and believe that He died for us, and humbly want, ask for and are willing to receive salvation . . . we get it." I carefully studied my man whom I knew had never heard anything like this before, for he had told me that when he did go to church it was to a super-nice, mentally-delicate type. This rugged, man-sized kind of religion was a new deal to him, but that it got to him was obvious.

"Only Jesus Christ can clean all the hate, the money grabbing, sexual, heavy drinking pattern and the dissatisfaction with life generally out of you. And He can if you've got the guts to come clean with Him and ask Him. So get down there on your knees by the window and look up at the cross and tell the Lord you are sorry for all the rottenness within yourself." This was pretty strong, I must admit, and I wouldn't take this approach except with certain people. This fellow was a real man, two fisted and had manlike treatment coming to him.

I judged him rightly, for he took my suggestion. In fact, he went all out for it, which no doubt explains why he got results. He fell to his knees and prayed about as follows (naturally, I didn't take his prayer down word for word, but it impressed me so forcibly that the following is just about verbatim; it was quite a prayer, believe me).

"Lord, I'm a louse, but You know that without my telling You. I'm a no-account bum, and if I started telling You all the dirt I've done, You would not have time to listen to anyone else, for You're pretty busy. Besides, You know all about me anyway, so how could I fool You?

"But believe me, God, I don't want to fool You. I'm sick of the lousy way I live and think and act. I don't want to be this way anymore. And that's the truth, too, God. I gotta admit that even as I talk I'm holding back a few reservations, but please don't let me be a phony. Help me to come clean as Dr. Peale says.

"I can't do anything about myself, so I put myself completely in Your hands. Let Your blood, which fell from the cross, fall over me now. I've just got to be changed."

I never heard anything like the way this man prayed when he got under way. He talked to the Lord with the same unmitigated honesty that he talked to me.

I have often wondered just what it was in the process that did the re-creative job on him, but have concluded that there were five factors: (1) He was fed up with what he was. (2) He wanted to be different, and he *really* wanted it. (3) He didn't mouth a lot of religious doubts and questions—he simply believed. (4) He took his religion straight, right out of the Bible, and this despite an Ivy League education and the softening done on him by an effete and swanky church background. (5) He went for it with all he had and so he got it. And he got the beginnings of it right then and there, too, though he had a long developing process ahead of him.

"Gosh, I feel better," he said standing up.

"You must have gotten some salvation already," I said, "for a half-hour ago you weren't saying gosh."

"Strange," he continued, "but that pent-up feeling is almost gone. I actually feel peaceful and sort of happy." His face had a look that impressed me. Had God touched him? That was the only possible explanation. Of course he wasn't changed from the worst to the best in this one conversation. A lot of spiritual work remained to be done on him, but the turn was taken, and even that small beginning brought relief and change.

Subsequently this man was able to work with fresh energy and vitality. And why not? Those unhealthy attitudes which had previously siphoned off his energy were gradually being overcome. His mind worked better and, as he put it when I saw him some months later, "So many new ideas pop out of my mind that I can't keep up with 'em."

Over a period of time I watched this man develop strength. He came alive spiritually, mentally and physically. He must have experienced "new birth," for he had, in effect, been born into a new world. New life energized him. Things do not now get him down as they did before that morning we met in the hotel restaurant. Now he really has what it takes to take it. And he takes things so well that he is moving ahead in personal affairs. This man became organized as he was re-activated around the dynamic God-center in his personality. That made of him a strong individual with a new competence for handling himself and his problems.

Actually being strong and having what it takes to take it is usually a matter of cultivation of your personality in spiritual depth. The dramatic and extreme revamping which I have just related is not required in most people. Basically they need only to believe that they can. And they can, too, if they persevere in this belief. If life is extra hard going for you, you had better have a real honest session with yourself and ask just where the trouble is. Maybe you are making it hard for yourself. The tendency is to blame other people or social conditions or forces beyond your control. But the real truth is that your problem is not beyond your control; the solution is within you. Emerson said, "There is always reason in the man for his good or bad fortune." Think that over carefully.

Failure must be traced, in the last analysis, to the presence of failure elements within the personality which have been allowed to dominate the thought pattern. These failure elements conspire to create within the mind a deep unconscious belief that you do not have the ability to succeed. And, as previously indicated, every human being tends to become what his mental image has habitually pictured him to himself as being.

The solution? Reverse the mental image. This of course will require considerable re-education of yourself and will not be easy. Creative achievement is never easy. But neither is it impossible. Actually, although difficult, the process is fairly simple in operation. It begins with realizing that your thinking should be corrected. That will go hard at first, for mental habits have channeled deep grooves in your consciousness, and your negative tendency will protest this strong positive mental reorientation. But if you are currently weak and defeated, it is due in large part to the fact that your mind has actually lied to you for years about your real abilities, trying to cause you to fail. So you must stand up to your mind. Personalize your mind and firmly tell it, "I have a powerful new thought, a vital faith thought and I intend to ride it to success and happiness and you—you old negative and defeatist thought pattern—you are through controlling me!" Don't ever let your mind control you. You always control it. And with God's help you can do just that. You can dominate your own mind if you strongly will to do so, and to that will, add the more dynamic motivating force of positive belief.

Young people were once taught this strong philosophy in the schools of America and in homes and churches, too. Such forthright teaching developed a great breed of men in this country, but it was rather generally abandoned and so a deteriorating softness set in. That was a crime against human nature, if you ask me. And I say that without being asked.

Memory takes me back to the old Williams Avenue School in Norwood, Ohio, a suburb of Cincinnati. My fifth grade teacher was George Reeves, a giant of a man at 240 pounds. I can still recall the forcible application of his huge hand to the seat of my trousers. Manual correction was regarded by him as beneficial to the student and contributory to the main purpose of education as he saw it, namely, to make men. And apparently these spankings took, for many years later I wrote a newspaper column about Mr. Reeves and how he had "licked" me. I must have received a score of letters from his former students in all parts of the country boasting that they, too, had been spanked by this man-sized teacher.

He was quite a character and he left a lasting impression upon the mind as well as the body. One of his methods which I recall was that, suddenly, in the midst of a class session he would thunder out, "Silence!" And when he ordered silence, I can assure you silence prevailed. He would then turn to the blackboard and write in large letters the word CAN'T. Then he would turn around and glare at us.

And we knew what to do. With united voice we would chant, "Strike the T off the CAN'T!" With a sweeping, powerful stroke he would erase the T, leaving the great word CAN standing forth unforgettably.

"Let that be a lesson to you," he would say. "Stop whining that you can't. Remember who you are. You are children of God. You are Americans. With God's help you can overcome all difficulties." Then he would add that phrase which I've never forgotten and never intend to forget. "You can if you think you can."

So it's just as simple as that. Strike the T off your CAN'T, and you will develop what it takes to take it. This is the way tough-minded optimists are made.

Don't write these suggestions off on the ground that you

are no longer a fifth grader or even a college undergraduate, or for that matter, even a young person. You are never too old to re-educate your mind from disbelief and self-doubt to belief and self-confidence.

I received a letter from a man 93 years old. He said, "I have had an inferiority complex for 93 years." If this is true, it is the longest inferiority complex that has ever come to my attention. "And it made me miserable for all those 93 years," he continued. "But a friend gave me your book, *The Power of Positive Thinking*. I read this book; I believed it; I practiced all your suggestions. And I'm writing to report the good news that after 93 years I have lost my inferiority complex."

And it would seem that he did, indeed, for in his concluding sentence he really comes through with some thorough-going positive thinking:

"The future looks good," he declared.

Another important factor in being strong enough to handle life forthrightly is to see in and beyond all difficulties the possibilities which are present. And, of course, possibilities are inherent in all difficult and seemingly unpropitious situations, though sometimes, to be sure, they are well concealed. The defeated mind can hardly bring success out of failure—for it is incapable of perceiving possibilities in hard situations. And even if such a mind might, perhaps, see some faint suggestion of opportunity, it does not have what it takes to bring it out.

But the strong person has a mind that is unclouded by shadowy gloom. He knows the score. He realizes full well the obstacles and resistances inherent in a given problem. But the quality about him that differentiates him from the defeated person is his ability always to see a chink of light in any darkness, however black.

I was reminded of people like this recently when my wife and I visited our daughter Elizabeth, a student at Mt. Holyoke College. Strolling about the campus we came to a sun dial on which is the following thought-provoking inscription: "To larger vision the end of shadow is the line of light."

What does that mean? Well once I took off from New York on a 707 Boeing Jet for Paris. It was near midnight, or five a.m. Paris time. It was a dark, moonless night and we leveled off at 33,000 feet. It was totally dark, but not for long. Looking east at that great height a very thin, almost infinitesimal line of light appeared on the far horizon where the shadow ended. A short time later and five hundred miles further on the radiant dawn flared up the heavens in all its glory.

The strong person has this "larger" vision and is therefore able to see the line of light at the end of the shadow. And he just never gives up either. One of the simplest things about all facts of life is that to get where you want to go, you must just keep on keeping on.

I was one of a group when the conversation turned on a certain man who was doing an unusual job under opposition and, of course, was the subject of jealousy-sparked criticism. He had a solid faith in his job and in himself and as I happen to know, in God also. Someone questioned whether he could stand up under all "the gaff." One man said "Don't worry about him. He's O.K. He never stops slugging."

This man came successfully through difficulty simply because he was an indomitable, dogged, determined, very resolute kind of personality. You can hardly help liking a man who slugs his way through, no matter what, regardless of what anybody says, or does, or doesn't do, so long as he knows that what he is doing is right, conscience clear, objectives worthy. This is tough-minded optimism in action.

It's quite wonderful to realize that you do not need to be weak, that you can be strong, that you can stand up to life, that you, too, can take it without folding up or being defeated.

How does one get this way? How do you develop this quality of having what it takes to take it? It is to develop the faith that God is no mere theoretical idea, but is actually near, and always helping you. Pray and think and practice this belief until you become absolutely sure that God is with you for a fact. Then you will know that when you have to face something hard, you do not have to meet it alone. God will see you through anything. God will be there to help you.

I was asked to call on a man in the hospital. Unexpectedly I walked into an inspiring experience. The sick man, a business leader from out of town, was very ill. Friends did not know whether he was fully aware of his condition.

"I heard you speak one night at a convention," he said. "You handed out some good stuff. Why did you come to see me? Busy as you are, you have no time to monkey around with an old invalid laid up on the shelf.

"You know what's wrong with me, don't you?" he asked straightforwardly. "I have cancer of the pancreas and I have about one chance in a thousand to live."

He seemed to want to talk, and went on to say, "I've never been any too religious, but don't believe I've been really bad. Never meant to anyway," he said in crisp sentences. "But I've been doing some thinking and I've got it all straightened out with God. I was brought up to believe in God, and I do one hundred per cent. Business associates have been writing me since I took sick, and you know, it's funny about those fellows. When I was associated with them in business they never once mentioned God, and now they are all talking God to me, and telling me that if I will have faith in God, He will see me through, no matter what happens. They tell me in their letters that they got through their own difficulties with God's help. Why don't they talk about God more in everyday life, I wonder?

"My father and mother taught me to put my faith in God. I

have a fight on my hands now, and I know it. But I think I'm on top of it, however the ball bounces. Whatever happens, God is with me. I can take it like a man and a Christian, I believe."

I sat looking at this man and finally said, "Do you know something? I will never forget you. I only hope I could demonstrate, under similar circumstances, half the courage and strength you show."

"You would," he said, "because you believe in God the same as I do, and if you ever get where I am, you can count on God. I've found, for a fact, that you can depend upon the Lord to help you take whatever you must."

He lived only four days after that visit, but had he gone on to be ninety he could hardly have attained greater manhood. This man went down through a valley which they sometimes call, the dark valley; but no valley through which he passed would be too dark, because there was a light about him and there were flags flying. You could almost hear the sound of trumpets as he passed over to the other side. He had what it takes to take it.

The creative thought principle is very important, for as Gautama Buddha declared, "The mind is everything; what you think you become."

If a person would start from childhood to build a sound spiritual thought pattern, it could make him almost proof against adversity and supply him with unshakeable strength throughout his life. But we have not built into our minds such a healthy thought world, and even our religion has too often contributed to a negative mental state.

As a spiritual teacher I have applied the principles of creative thought control to many of my students and the success percentage in overcoming personal weakness has been quite high.

For example, one night, a year or so ago, I was flying to the West Coast, and a man sat with me for much of the flight, who was not only quite out of strength but sick of body, mind and soul as well.

He described in detail his physical symptoms—obesity, high blood pressure, shortness of breath, nervous stomach, liver acting up, pains in some joints. Unwittingly he opened up and displayed an acutely diseased mind as well. As he poured out his sick thoughts they were a miserable compound of resentment, hate, jealousy, pessimism, and lust. He was living a life of low-grade morality, to state it mildly.

After regaling me for a couple of hours time and a thousand miles of distance with this putrid mess of thoughts, he suddenly asked "What in the h . . . do you think is wrong with me?"

"Your reference to hell," I replied thoughtfully, "may be more significant than you intended. It could just be that you are in the shape you're in because actually you are in a state of hell. In other words, your trouble is bad thoughts, very bad thoughts. And remember, please, that bad thoughts like yours can make you sick, really sick, by externalizing themselves as physical symptoms."

"Bad thoughts—you think that's my trouble, eh?" mused my seatmate. "Why hasn't some writer or teacher or preacher made it clear long before now how wrong thinking can have such bad effects, and what to do about it?"

"Some of us have tried to," I replied, "but let's skip the past and do something constructive now. Here is my suggestion and don't think it won't help you for it will. Start tomorrow to read the first four books of the New Testament—Matthew, Mark, Luke, John. Underscore every sentence that impresses you as a healthy thought. Continue this reading and underscoring, not missing one single day.

"And as you read and underscore, also commit each selected

passage, memorizing it so that you can repeat these passages easily without the book. Say them over and over, savoring their melody and meaning, and at the same time visualizing these thoughts as sinking deeply into your mind to cancel out those old rotten, bad thoughts which have been poisoning your consciousness and undermining your health."

One example I gave him was Matthew 6:22; 23 (Rev. Standard) "The eye is the lamp of the body. So, if your eye is sound, your whole body will be full of light; but if your eye is not sound, your whole body will be full of darkness."

"This means," I explained, "that the way you see things, the attitude you take, the slant of your thinking determines whether your whole being shall be full of darkness and gloom, or light and joy. It's how you see or look upon life that makes the difference."

You never know for sure whether your lessons take, but this man seemed responsive. I shook hands with him at the West Coast airport, and he vanished out of sight and memory too. But months later in a Chicago hotel lobby, a man walked up to me. "Do you remember me?" he asked. This is often a difficult question when one moves about meeting as many people as I do, but I always answer it without evasion. "You do look familiar, but I must confess I don't know you."

"I'm not surprised," he replied, "though I spent a night with you once. But then I was a broken down, overfat, washed up sort of slob."

"Well, that description certainly doesn't fit you now," I said, looking admiringly upon the trim, clean-cut, healthy looking person in front of me.

Then I remembered him—"I know you," I exclaimed. "You're the man with the bad thoughts."

"Was, you mean, but no more," he said with a grin. "I really went to work on that Bible plan of yours. I now know a lot of Scripture passages, and they are packed down in my consciousness as you said. My mind is solidly full of them. And they healed my mind too—there is absolutely no doubt of it, and I feel better all over. In fact, I'm disgustingly healthy, and," he added, "I've found a strength and vigor that I hadn't felt in years. And I've had some tough times this past year. Things happened that would have floored me completely. Now, with the Lord's guidance and help, I have what it takes to take it and even more, to do something with it."

The method which proved so successful in this case can work wonders for you also. But sometimes a profounder therapy is indicated; a healing deep within the personality structure, or to state it another way, a fundamental change of radical nature is required. Over the years it is quite possible to build up inwardly a body of failure in the form of conflict and stress. This manifests itself in various reactions which add up to defeatism. But there is a cure.

Let me tell you the curious story of one unhappy man whose healing of personality is one of the strangest human dramas I have ever known.

This man, a capable person, was for years victim of some glaring personality defects. He was overly tense, to an extent that made everyone around him tense. He was a perfectionist, insisting that everything be done exactly so, and immediately. When he came to his office, his employees instinctively tensed up. If the slightest thing went wrong he would "hit the ceiling," and from what I gathered he circulated around the ceiling most of the time.

At home he was, if anything, even more demanding. In the office he at least made a feeble attempt to be polite, but at home he really let himself go. Though no doubt he loved his wife, he had, without realizing it, made her the shock-absorber of his irritations, and of these he had plenty. He would swear and shout and carry on and pick up anything that wasn't nailed down and hurl it. Then he would slump into deep, dark depression and remain in it for hours, or even days.

Year after year the wife patiently put up with this behavior. She was devoted to her husband, indeed to her he was a great man, and her job in life was to make things as easy as possible for him, so she reasoned. She prayed for strength to endure his outbursts and got it, but gradually the constant pressure began to siphon off her energy, and he was increasingly hard to take.

Then one fine evening the worm turned, as the saying goes. The man had seethed into one of his tirades when suddenly the wife turned on him in flashing fury. Eyes blazing, walking the floor as she talked, she began pouring out to him the unvarnished facts of just what his personality looked like to her and others. When he tried to interject a protest, she snapped, "Keep still and listen! I've endured your tirades for years; now it's your turn to listen, and believe me, you're going to listen."

As he sat helplessly taking in the devastating picture of himself she was drawing for him, this man suddenly had a strange experience. His wife's voice seemed to fade. It was as though he were alone and gazing into a slowly moving stream. Somehow he realized that it was the stream of his personality he was seeing into. It was like a slowly flowing river and in midstream a large, rough looking, dark hard object was ponderously bobbing up and down. This he recognized as a big lump of sin, his sin, a composite of all the trouble factors deep within him—guilt, hate, uncontrolled tension.

This experience may indeed be a sharp insight into the basic trouble of many people. Do we have separate sins and weaknesses and evils, or are they manifestations of a central sin, weakness or evil? Perhaps they are but manifestations of one big, hard, lumpy, hidden sin imbedded in consciousness and from which is sent off individual and viewable weaknesses. It could very well be that sin is indivisible and that essentially we have not sins, but sin. Get that central sin broken up and drained off, and you will be changed.

As suddenly as it came, the strange vision passed, and there before him was his wife, still talking. All at once he felt very tender toward her and sorry for all the bad times he had given her. Apparently perceiving that something unusual had happened to him, she looked at him strangely, stopped speaking, and sank into a chair, exhausted.

He knew then that he would have to change. He was afraid if he didn't do something quickly about that hard, lumpy thing in his stream of consciousness, his personality would close over and he would continue as he had been. The thought came that only God could change him, for he knew very well he could do nothing for himself. He told his wife about what he had seen and together they prayed intensely imploring God to help him.

In telling of his experience, he emphasized the intensity of their petition, explaining that he had never before appealed to God with "everything he had," as he did then. "Suddenly I felt faith burst in my mind. In that instant I believed. You have no idea of the feeling of relief that came over me."

No dramatic immediate transformation took place, but that he wasn't the same man was obvious and the change was steady. He became quieter, less intense, even calm, and certainly more controlled. He was able to achieve significant improvement in his thinking and acting. His change indicates that the hard lump had broken up and floated off. And indeed it must be so, for the wife, who certainly ought to know, says with a look of wonder in her eyes, "My husband is so different."

The practical results have been quite definite. He tells of a new and astonishing feel of strength and power. "The horrible pressure that used to build up in me is gone, and I feel much relieved. Why didn't someone tell me of this power long before I messed up my life so badly? Well, anyway, thank God I know about it now."

You really can develop strength and have it takes to take it. You can become a tough-minded optimist.

Sum-up of *Have What It Takes To Take It*

1. To live in this world you just have to be strong—or else. So start developing inner toughness or tensile strength of mind and spirit.

2. When the going gets tough, let the tough get going— you're tough.

3. Constantly re-emphasize to yourself the great fact that God built potential strength into your nature. By affirming it and practicing it, this basic strength will toughen up as muscles do.

4. Get yourself changed spiritually for real strength is not truculence. It is rather a God-like power reaction in which strong Christ-like gentleness is an important factor.

5. Reverse your mental image of yourself as being *weak* to a clear picture of yourself as becoming *strong*. Then hold that concept firmly in consciousness until it takes with you.

6. Practice until you master it; then keep practicing to keep it, the powerful creative thought that you can if you think you can.

7. Become a possibilitarian. No matter how dark things seem to be or actually are, raise your sights and see the possibilities—always see them, for they're always there.

8. Know for a fact that with God's help you can take what you have to take like a man.

9. Remember: what you think you will become—good or bad, weak or strong, defeated or victorious.

TWO

NEVER BE AFRAID OF
ANYBODY OR ANYTHING

"Never be afraid of anybody or anything in this life." I remember that statement as though it were yesterday. The speaker was Grove Patterson, the place the editorial office of the old *Detroit Journal*, the time October, 1920.

As a young reporter just out of college I was getting a briefing from my boss who subsequently was to become a life-long friend. He pointed a blunt, inky finger at me. He seemed always to have ink on his fingers. "Listen to me, Norman, and never forget it. Don't go through life shaking in your shoes and skulking from a bunch of fears. What the heck is there to be afraid of?"

Guess he read me pretty well, for fear and shrinking inferiority troubled and plagued me for years until I learned how to get over it. And this lecture by Grove Patterson was important in that educational process.

"Stand up to people and to things. Look them in the eye and tell them all to go jump. Say to yourself, and say it every day, enough times to make it stick: 'With God's help I will not be afraid of anybody or anything.'"

My editor really got to me that day. He drove his words

and his own man-size faith into my consciousness. For the first time I had a ray of hope that I could lick my fears. Seeming to read my mind he added a few more potent words and the battered old newspaper office on Jefferson Avenue lighted up with them. To this day I recall the power I felt as Grove slowly recited: "Be strong and of a good courage; be not afraid, neither be thou dismayed: for the Lord thy God is with thee whithersoever thou goest." (Jos. 1:9)

Giving me a friendly whack he said, "Get out there now, old boy, and give it all you've got!" It was one of those experiences you always return to in memory to draw new vitality for living.

Since that time I have worked overtime on the mastery of fear. At first I was motivated by a very personal reason; I was sick and tired of being afraid, shy, and nervous. I simply had to find relief and release or else. I just wasn't going to go through life suffering the torment of fear. I couldn't live with it and so was determined to live without it.

But how? That was the big question. Grove Patterson said religious faith would help me. Well, I was a religious young fellow of sorts; my father was a preacher and I had been immersed in church all my life until I went to college. Then for four years, I'm ashamed to say, I scarcely ever went to church except when my parents came to visit me. Maybe I'd had too much church or perhaps the preachers in the college church didn't reach me, though I gave them very little chance, I must say.

When at home on vacation I went every Sunday to hear my father preach. But he was different. It was manly down-to-earth, practical stuff that he put out and he clearly showed that he loved the people sitting out front. He had been a doctor of medicine in his early days and he must have been a good doctor, too, judging from the practice and position he had in Milwaukee where he had his office. Then following a serious illness he experienced a remarkable spiritual conversion and couldn't stay out of the ministry. He always wrapped medicine and religion together into a kind of body, mind and soul package. He believed in the Bible and in spiritual experience and was at the same time an alert liberal thinker with a strong social awareness.

He was unique in thought, expression and method and distinctly was cast in no ordinary mold. He was a complete individualist. As I listened to him and lived with him, too, I realized that he had something different, very different: a Christianity that really worked with a powerful, therapeutic, mind-changing force. I clearly saw that as the mind is healed so also are body and soul affected. And I grasped the further tremendous truth that many of the ills of human beings, both of mind and body, originate in soul sickness.

From my father's practical religious emphasis I began to see that there was a way out of my own conflicts. This started me on the search for peace of mind, for victory over myself, and for the strength and power I was sure Christianity offered. I did not find it at once; indeed it was a long and often frustrating search but I found enough so that, like my father before me, I too felt a definite call to the ministry.

I entered Boston University School of Theology but did not find there the answer to my own problem which I was still seeking. The first attempt of the faculty was to upset my "simple" faith and to substitute an intellectualized approach to the teachings of Jesus which made of them a kind of social manifesto. They called this the "social Gospel" approach, meaning the application of Christ's teachings to the problems of society. It was considered much superior to the seemingly antiquated "individual Gospel" or the saving of men's souls and minds. There was little effort to balance each important emphasis, the individual and social, as being included in a "whole or complete Gospel." But I was impressed by the

faculty, the church leaders, the extra-smart students; and I became an enthusiastic exponent of the so-called social Gospel.

However, after a few years of preaching this exclusive social
emphasis, I began to grow skeptical of it as the answer of
answers. What personal spiritual insight and strength I had
was beginning to grow thin and stale. Also the plain people
who came to my church seemed to be reached and gripped
only when I talked with them, in a simple manner, about
God's way to a better life. I began to question whether the
social-ethical type of Christianity actually possessed the dynamic of personality change. I realized that individuals needed
God in their personal lives before they would support God-
centered social programs. And under the exclusive emphasis
on this social Gospel I saw people deteriorating in their personal spiritual lives.

So being in a sincere dilemma I found myself thumbing over
the New Testament page by page hoping to find definite pro-
gramming of this social Gospel. I was naive enough to believe
the New Testament to be our only really authoritative and
basic document about what Jesus Christ really teaches. But
my scholarly friends told me not to look there but rather to
some vague source which they called "the best insights of our
time."

I was greatly impressed by this superior wisdom (a hangover
of my old fear of people—I've always been awed by scholars
and the glib-tongued) and sought my answer in these so-called
"best insights." But presently I began to ask questions: Who
has these insights and what do they know anyway? And I
realized further that even best insights may change with the
passing of time while "Jesus Christ (is) the same yesterday,
and today, and for ever." (Heb. 13:8)

I finally concluded that His teachings are primarily designed
to develop Godly people out of this evil world. These Godly
people would, if sufficiently de-paganized, have attitudes of

concern for their fellow men. They would practice brother-hood and hold all men in esteem regardless of race, color or position. They would try to make life better for everyone, especially "these little ones" (Mark 9:42) meaning the weak and unfortunate. I saw that the principles of enlightened society grew out of such basic teachings. But I just never could go along with the bumptious assumption that to be a Christian I had to lead a strike or join a socialist party or push social legislation through congress or call people reactionaries who didn't do so. I noticed how cocky and often downright mean the extremists were in both the liberal and fundamental-ist camps and so I decided I would travel down the middle road with average sensible people who didn't have all the answers and who realized that fact but who were humbly seeking God.

I graduated from Theology School and took a church in Brooklyn which had only forty members and a tumbledown little frame structure. Enthusiastically, I went out into the growing community in the effort to build up the church. I climbed stairways, pounded pavements and used every means at my disposal to reach people; and one by one brought them in until, in less than three years, we had nearly a thousand members and a fine new building. I kept trying to establish a synthesis of the social and individual Gospel message always emphasizing what a wonderful thing life can be when organ-ized around Christ and surrendered to God. And we had a wonderful happy congregation of people but happy in a truly dedicated way. My father's dynamic faith was getting through to them even through me, strangely enough, who was surely one of the most uncertain instruments God ever used.

Then I was called to a big beautiful church in Syracuse—a glorious structure constructed almost entirely of huge mag-nificent windows set in stone. I can visualize even now how on bright Sunday mornings the sun streamed through the art glass driving long shafts of light down the massive pillar-lined nave.

It was a university pulpit and, still awed by scholars, especially by some who affected profundity, I delivered some real "intellectual" sermons. Then one of the professors, Dean Bray, a kindly man and a true scholar, took me to lunch one day and said, "Don't try to impress us with scholarship. Though we are professors we are human beings first, believe it or not. You are our spiritual teacher; break the bread of life to us in pieces small enough that we can digest them. Simply be yourself and share with us in our need what God means to you and has done for you personally. Show us the way to peace, to understanding and to strength." Wise advice from a professor great enough to be simple.

Well, the trouble was that I had just about lost what spiritual vitality I had possessed. And it wasn't only that. Those old fears and pesky self-doubts still plagued me, and I was getting more tense and conflicted in mind and emotion. My religion, I had to admit, was not of sufficient depth, vitality or penetration to heal my long-established traumatic condition of mind. The super-duper ethical and sociological pattern that passed for Christianity and which, indeed, had come to dominate American liberal Protestantism was to me just plain unsatisfying and ineffective. If it couldn't change me, one person, how could it change anything, let alone society? I simply had to find something that would really work, or else. And I knew where to look for it, too.

I began a serious scientific study of people who had experienced definite and profound changes in their personalities: former drunks, thieves, libertines; and troubled people of all kinds who were now entirely free of their former difficulty. I found in almost every case it was an in-depth surrender to Jesus Christ that had brought about amazing changes.

While none of the problems mentioned above were mine,

I had some other difficulties that were equally as complicated and misery-producing. I had fear, shyness, self-doubt, feelings of inadequacy and a big inferiority complex. Could the act of surrender to Jesus Christ cleanse all this mess of weakness out of me as it had for the people studied? I really believed that it could though I had never heard anything about it at Boston University except from dear old "Daddy" Butters, a very human type of professor, who would drop in on the students for talks and pray with them and ask in kindly fashion, "Are you being 'good boys'?"

But I found I couldn't avail myself fully of this salvation in the years following my graduation from the seminary until I got over an intellectual hurdle. It seemed that this business of being "saved" or "changed" was generally looked upon askance by intellectualized Christian leaders and my association with them caused me to shy away from it too. In fact it was almost considered "corny." At least life-changing wasn't being stressed in the "best" circles; and as for sin, apparently that was only social phenomena confined to capitalists and Republicans, as contrasted with the saintly labor leaders and left wing, super-sophisticated politicians. You hardly ever heard about sin from super-up-to-the-minute preachers, save in a theoretical sense; except from the few remaining "reactionaries" who still had their doubts about socialism and they soon were made to realize they were no longer in the inner circle of the controlling ecclesiastical leaders.

Revival meetings such as those held by Billy Sunday, and more recently by Billy Graham (and the intellectuals have little use for him), were looked down the nose at. The whole idea of revival fell into disuse in liberal Christianity. How many times have I watched Bill Jones and Mary Smith and Harry Wilson, plain everyday college graduates, doing their best to be inspired by the spiritless, though erudite, lifeless Christianity in which they tried to find interest. In short, the heart and lots of the soul went out of Christianity, and as that happened thousands headed straight for hell though they maintained the outward forms and even came to church and contributed to the budget.

In my mind I roamed far and wide in an attempt to find a system of faith and a method for practicing that faith that would give me a personal victory over myself. Before I could ever help other people to victory I had to find it for myself else it would be another case of the blind leading the blind and both going into the ditch.

I began reading certain spiritual literature which I had become aware was increasingly pouring into the homes of people in the churches and reaching them, too, with its message. This material came from the Unity Movement, from Science of Mind, from various metaphysical teachers, from Christian Science, the Oxford group and Moral Rearmament. Glen Clark, Starr Daily and Sam Shoemaker were eagerly read authors. These writers taught that Jesus Christ established a scientific, completely workable way of thought and life that brought about change and victory. What I read was in a sense reminiscent of my father's preaching, though he never had access to any of these writings in his earlier years. He had arrived at somewhat similar concepts by his own independent search for a practical and specific message for modern human beings that would really work when needed.

A loyal minister in the oldest church in this land, the Reformed Church in America, I always was and still am an orthodox Christian. I believe in the Bible as the word of God as sincerely as the most dyed-in-the-wool fundamentalist, apart from the stilted vocabulary and mechanistic approach some of them insist upon. I accept completely the plan of salvation. I believe that Jesus Christ is the Divine Son of God and our Lord and Saviour. I believe in the Holy Spirit, the Virgin Birth of Christ and, indeed, in all the statements of the Apos-

tles' Creed. I go right down the line with the historic doc-
trines of the Christian Church but I also believe that this
ancient faith can be taught in new and fresh thought and
language forms and applied scientifically and with creative
power in people's lives; that it can solve the toughest problems of human nature and society, too.

This I have taught in my sermons and books not without
considerable opposition from some ministers. A few have even
preached sermons against me referring to my teachings as
"Pealism"—the liberals condemning me for one reason, the
fundamentalists for another. But I have rediscovered the old
saying, and it really works: "Every knock is a boost."

An amusing illustration of this was when a group of my
church members at a meeting were in turn telling what had
brought them to our church. One woman said, "The devil
brought me to Marble Collegiate Church." She chuckled as
she said it—which relieved the startled people listening. She
explained by saying, "I was a member of Pastor _____'s church
and he was always preaching against Pastor Peale 'as of the
devil.' He harped on this awful Pastor Peale so much that I became curious and went to Pastor Peale's church. I found people waiting in line to attend services. I listened to the sermon
and it seemed good Biblical gospel to me and I attended for several Sundays. Then I went back to my own church and Pastor
_____ was still preaching against Pastor Peale. So I went up to
him after the sermon and asked him, 'Are there perhaps two
Pastor Peales?' 'No,' he replied, 'there is only one, Norman
Vincent Peale.' 'Well,' I said, 'it's very strange. I've been listening to his sermons and he isn't at all like you say he is.' He
got red in the face," she reported, and added: "I decided to
join Pastor Peale's church."

Apparently these good men did not like anyone to talk
Christianity in any other terminology or thought forms than
those which they traditionally employed. Though I am sure

they were sincere in their ideas it apparently seemed repre-
hensible for anyone to be at all different in method and approach: we must all be in the same mould, it appeared. Perhaps the fact that this type of spiritual teaching was reaching
great numbers of people may have bothered them.

I have never taken exception to disagreement nor until now
did I refer to unkind and sarcastic remarks such as, for example, the less than gracious—shall we call it—statement of
Rev. Robert F. Fitch, Dean of the Pacific School of Religion
who for such a distinguished scholar referred to me somewhat
inelegantly as a "pap dispenser" and further declared, "Peale's
stuff is pure magic about as totally divorced from genuine
Christian religion as you can get."

In this connection I must admit I was comforted by a
kindly, earthy, remark by an old mining engineer, who sent
me some of these remarks as reported by the *Denver Post*. This
mining engineer must be a delightful character and a real
thinker. He commented: "Dr. Bob Fitch should ask the Almighty some questions. Having worked all my life with professors of geology I've found that having a doctor's degree
doesn't mean a hell of a lot." (Rather on the rough side, no
doubt, but sound. At any rate it warmed my heart against misunderstanding.)

Having always had sincere respect for our church leaders
and heads of schools of theology and professors, I had been
hurt by their violent attacks upon me. Strangely enough these
attacks were not only on my ideas but upon me as a person.
I've often wondered why some ministers can become so very
bitter. I am sorry to say it, but some of the meanest things ever
said, in my experience, and the crudest and most impolite remarks have come not from laymen or ignorant and uncultured
people, but from educated ministers of the Gospel. One
wonders if some may unknowingly have bottled up hate and
antagonism which they empty out in erudite ministerial lan-

guage, seldom as vulgarly phrased as Fitch's remark but full of barbs nevertheless. Especially virulent, it seems, is this strange hostility when aroused by a brother minister. This reference is to only a few and to a certain type. Ministers generally are lovable, earnest gentlemen, and I honor them sincerely.

But I simply decided to take it; to pray for my detractors; and try to act like a Christian. Despite a hostile attitude toward me I continued to respect these gentlemen for their otherwise effective leadership and never had ill will toward any of them personally. I definitely tried to practice my own teachings, one of which is never to tolerate within my mind any hateful attitude toward another person.

But even so, still a bit awed by ecclesiastical influence and authority, I was cut to the quick by their attacks, so much so that at one time I actually decided to resign from the ministry and carry on my work of helping people outside the organized church. I had even written my resignation. I am amazed now that I ever let these men affect me; they don't any more, that's for sure. But several things deterred me from leaving the church. One was the friendly understanding of my denomination, The Reformed Church in America, which you will pardon me for characterizing as one of the most balanced, truly free and substantial Christian bodies in our country. Another was the friendship of the leaders and members, and the tremendous throng of visitors crowding Marble Collegiate Church to hear proclaimed the simple life-changing power of God. Countless lives were being changed; God was blessing this ministry and I knew I simply had to keep preaching this message from the pulpit of the oldest church in America to keep faith with the Lord and needy people.

Another reason was simply that I felt I was right. I was constantly seeking God's guidance and when you feel you are right you are then given courage and support. Always in my prayers the Lord seemed to tell me to go right on helping His people with His Gospel in language they could understand and with practical methods they could take hold of and use; and to ignore the attacks of men.

A final reason I did not resign and work outside the church was my father, at the time an old man but as alert mentally and spiritually as ever. He said, "Norman, I have read and studied all your books and sermons and it is clearly evident that you have gradually evolved a new religious system of thought and teaching. And it's O.K., too, very O.K., because its center and circumference and essence is Jesus Christ. There is no doubt about its solid Biblical orientation. Yes, you have evolved a new Christian emphasis out of a composite of Science of Mind, metaphysics, Christian Science, medical and psychological practice, Baptist evangelism, Methodist witnessing and solid Dutch Reformed Calvinism."

I disparaged his statement that I had produced anything at all new. Who am I to develop a new type of Christianity? I'm no theologian, merely a preacher and pastor. "It's just the old Gospel that I teach, Dad," I said, "in present day vocabulary and thought forms."

"That is true," he declared. "But it's never been done before in just this way and to this extent. Your work is a synthesis of the old and the new and never at any time have you been other than faithful to Jesus Christ and the Bible. You teach the whole gospel of sin, conviction, redemption, atoning grace and salvation, but you have simplified it and made it a practical and joyous way of life. It is absolutely Christ-centered and persons are its objective."

"But, Dad," I said, "some of these important ecclesiastics and some who aren't so important but invariably take their cue from the leaders are really after my skin. I have actually felt like resigning and setting up my ministry outside the church."

He looked long at me. "That would break my heart. You are a true preacher of Jesus Christ and true to the church. Take that from an old preacher and besides," he added, "the Peales never quit." That did it. I stayed in the church. And there is room in God's great church for differing types of men and varying approaches if the teaching is true to Jesus Christ.

I could print hundreds of letters from hard working, sincere, everyday pastors and plain folk from everywhere who have assured me of the effectiveness of our pattern of thought and practice as it has actually worked out in their lives and in their churches, too. The purpose of this chapter is not to defend myself or my message but rather to outline how some of us have found the secret of never being afraid of anyone or anything. The following letter may serve as a sample:

There were so many frightening things wrong with me. I had an ulcer and my hands and knees were paralyzed at public functions. After two years of therapy, I gave it up—still with an active ulcer and muscles that refused to co-ordinate.

Since college I had decided religion was only for weaklings; now I realized I was one of these. I had been groping. When the war ended, I had gone from one Protestant church to another until I found one with an open door where I could sit and say an inarticulate thank you. I read William James' *Varieties of Religious Experience,* the only argument I found that explained the intellectual validity of religion. Then, in a library, I found a couple of your books. With the greatest difficulty and reluctance and fear, I told God I was giving myself entirely over to Him.

It has taken a number of years but from the time I read your books, the circumstances of our living changed. Our quiet desperation became a subtle hope. I found a doctor who helped the ulcer—another who diagnosed my rigid constriction. My husband's business problem was worked out, our children's behavioral difficulties eased. My husband is employee counselor for a nation-wide industry. He is a church deacon and Sunday School Superintendent. I am a library director, our son has a fellowship for summer work at his medical school, and our daughter has been accepted at a good college.

I know you must disregard the criticism of some of the clergy who seem to infer that your religion is not deep enough for it is only by its simplicity and practicality that it is made available to dazed, lost and sick souls.

I found that a basic factor in living without fear is to hold and practice the simple belief that God will take care of you. This conviction was for me an important foundation stone in building courage.

A friend, Albert E. Cliffe, a prominent chemist in Canada, was on his deathbed and hope for his life had been given up. In that moment of dire need he surrendered himself to God saying, "I give myself to you, O Lord. Do with me as you will." He achieved that amazing separation from self which is so vital to spiritual change. He felt new peace and strength. He got well and for many years lived an extraordinarily fruitful life.

He was teacher of one of the large Bible classes in his city. He wrote a book with the provocative title *Let Go and Let God*—a volume to which I owe a great personal debt. The title itself is a creative-living formula. As a chemist he was constantly dealing with formulas and this spiritual formula was in his opinion as exact as any in his scientific work. This formula was designed and used to break the strain of trouble or fear by simply turning a problem or difficulty or fear over to God, then mentally seeing or visualizing it as released to God.

I became very impressed with Al Cliffe's formula, the more so because of the amazing effect it had upon his life and upon my own and many others also. So, when a fear began to take hold of my thoughts, I would simply say, "Let go and let God." I would practice the mental attitude that it was now completely out of my hands and made myself willing to accept whatever the Lord's will for me might be. This procedure, as I found, does not come easily; but it does come, provided you work diligently at it. In so doing you will gradually become proficient in the spiritual skill of letting go—all hate, all selfishness, all fear.

This technique of full relinquishment is sometimes referred to by the term "surrender" which involves the active, deliberate mental giving up of the fear of whatever trouble to God. This, of course, is anything but easy, for the mind tends to hold tightly even to that from which it actually craves release. Charles Dickens wrote a line which always fascinates me by its subtle understanding of this psychological fact: "We wear the chains we forge in life." We do indeed form the links one by one in a chain of fear until we are bound by it and, strangely enough, we love, even as we hate, our chains. This curious mental equivocation explains, in part at least, why it is so difficult to rid ourselves of our fears on our own.

It has been demonstrated repeatedly, however, that when a person actually makes up his mind that he wants an end to his fear, and honestly admits he can do nothing about it himself and surrenders it completely to God, release comes in a most astonishing manner.

And, believe me, I know whereof I speak. I personally discovered this way out from fear and it was a hard way. I had made some progress in scientific spiritual living during my Syracuse days. But when I moved to New York City, back in 1932, the old fears that had plagued me from boyhood again ganged up on me. I was now pastor of a famous church on Fifth Avenue and some people were saying that I was too young and inexperienced for so responsible a post—that I just didn't have what it takes. Though in my heart, I couldn't gainsay these depreciatory appraisals, still the remarks goaded me to "show" them that I could handle the job, no matter what they said. This was not what might be called the highest of motives but I was never one to take a licking without giving it an awfully good try.

But problems added up. It was the time of the great depression. People were tramping streets looking for jobs which were all but non-existent. It was the lowest period economically and psychologically in the United States I have ever seen in my lifetime. Nothing before or since that I have experienced has even remotely approached the depth of discouragement which rested upon the American people, especially in a financial center like New York.

Added to these dismal social and business conditions, the congregation of the church to which I had come was reduced to very small number; and in the large sanctuary, it seemed I was talking to only a dispirited handful. In raising a budget it was all we could do to get together $15,000 in annual contributions from the congregation of this noted Fifth Avenue Church, the oldest continuing Protestant congregation in America.

The church was really in low spirits and so was I. The old fears grabbed my mind with their icy fingers. Whatever was I going to do? Failure, grim failure stared me in the face! My mind went around in desperate circles, leaving me ever more tense and discouraged and consequently relatively ineffective.

At this point summer vacation time came and Mrs. Peale and I went off on a long-planned trip to Europe. But instead of being thrilled by the trip I poured a constant stream of negative, fear-filled conversation into her ears. She is a loving, patient wife and she listened. Indeed that was about all she could do! My ceaseless flow of talk limited her conversational opportunity, to say the least.

Finally, after arriving in England and some days of rather unhappy wandering, we came to the town of Keswick in the heart of the English Lake District. The Keswick Station Hotel was a typical English country inn. Its halls and staircases were lined with prints and huge somber paintings of Lake District scenes and the largest collection of pewter I had ever seen.

The hotel had a glorious English formal garden and from its walks one had magnificent views of the stern, cloud-shrouded, encompassing hills. During the "bright intervals," hopefully mentioned daily in weather forecasts, a light and glory would burst through the clouds and, for a time, fully illume the flowers, hedges and well-clipped lawns, the like of which you see only in England.

At the far end of the garden was a bench. It is still there today. We go back now and then and sit there and give thanks to God. For on that summer day in 1933 I found the basic secret of not being afraid of anybody or anything and have since been privileged to teach that formula to thousands of people, many of whom have likewise been set free from the domination of fear.

As we sat together on that bench that afternoon I again started the dismal recital of my fears. I told Ruth for the thousandth time how discouraging everything was, how tough it was going to be back home. I listed my problems, all of them seemingly so formidable. I expressed my complete assurance of failure.

Then it happened, one of the top experiences of my life, the beginning of a thrilling adventure in personal change and unexpected but notable victory over fear. My wife Ruth is a gentle, kindly soul but when she gets aroused and becomes firm, brother, she is really firm. Turning to me she said,

"Please stop this negative talk. I've heard enough of it. What are you—a phony? You *teach* faith—haven't you any yourself? Or are you only a lot of meaningless words? Doesn't God and Jesus Christ mean anything to you?

"God has given you great potential ability and has called you to unprecedented opportunity for service. You are equal to it if only you will forget yourself. All you think of is yourself—you are involved, tied up, dominated by yourself. And so you walk in gloom and fear until life is hardly worth it. I am so very sorry for you."

Then she took my hand in her smaller hand. How soft I always thought it was on moonlight walks, but it wasn't soft now. It had a powerful grip on mine and she said firmly, "You are going to sit right here with me on this bench until you surrender yourself, and your fears, to Jesus Christ."

Then I, who was her pastor, who had been educated in theology, meekly asked, "But how does one surrender? What do I do and say? How can I let go?"

I can hear her yet speaking out of the native wisdom of the truest heart I've ever known. She said simply, "Say dear Lord I now give myself, my life, my mind, my body, my soul to You. I give You all my fears. If You want me to fail I am willing to accept failure. Whatever You do with me is all right with me. Take all of me. I surrender everything to You."

Haltingly I repeated the words after Ruth and in that moment I meant what I was saying, really meant it. That prayer went down deeply into my mind, and came up with the truth, with absolute truth. Suddenly all tension and unhappiness went out of me. I could literally feel it go like a stretched rubber band returning to normal. A sense of happiness—joy is a better word—such as I had never felt before in my life surged through my whole being. I had never felt anything like it in my entire experience.

The relief I felt was so intense, so overwhelming as actually to be painful, like a deep wound emptying itself of infection; but that sensation soon gave way to one of indescribable relief. If I never have it again I had it once: a sense of God's healing Presence so powerful and unmistakable, so real, that I knew for a certainty that He is and does touch our weak human lives with His amazing grace and power.

Had I not had this extraordinary experience I am certain that my life would have been all but ruined by fear, inferiority feelings, and a crippling failure obsession. I realized then that not only I but thousands of similarly beset people could be set free from fear, that terrible destroyer, through the simple formula of surrender. I knew further that this was my mission in life, to explain and urge upon my fellow men a method of faith and practice literally packed with power, the power to live beyond the frustrations and defeats of self and of the world as well.

There are, of course, other factors of importance in knowing how never to be afraid of anybody or anything; but the basic, primary, and completely essential step is that of surrender, of letting go and letting God. Fundamentally this is not something you can do for yourself—only God can really do it for you. And God can and will when you really allow Him to control the whole action of your mind and its capacity to believe.

Such intense spiritual experiences as I have described are very rare. Why they come, to whom they come, and when, only God knows; and each is a blessing which I would hesitate to try to analyze. The usual method for gaining release from fear is through a long and persistent application of the laws of the spiritual life as outlined in scientific religious practice.

One of these laws is what has been called the practice of the Presence of God. The most important fact of all facts in this world is that we, you and I, are not alone. The whole business of life on earth would be pretty futile if there were no God to give meaning and purpose to it. We would be not unlike frightened children lost in a dark and fearful forest. Some might display a bit of bravado but all would be pretty well scared and rightly so.

But it is not enough to believe theoretically that there is a God. This belief in itself will never free you from fear until, by spiritual emphasis and practice, you gain an unmistakable, deeply personal conviction of a guiding and supporting Presence and confidently live by it.

And how is this accomplished? Well, let me tell you about a man whom I met one night when I made a talk in a southern city before some two thousand salesmen. I was talking about self-confidence and integrated personality and, naturally, I stressed the importance of mastering fear.

After I had finished my talk a man came backstage and introduced himself as the owner of a thriving small business in the community. I could see at once that he was a dynamic and assured person.

"How right you are about faith and positive thinking," he said. And he proceeded to tell me about himself. "Some years ago," he continued, "I was in a difficult situation. Business was in bad shape and my state of mind was even worse. I was a victim of fear, self-doubt, and indecision. Through your books I took to reading the Bible and, for the first time in my life, I learned to pray. One day I made a deal with the Lord."

Made a deal with the Lord? . . . Now when he said that, I shrank back a little because I am always suspicious of such talk. The phrase is not a happy one and neither is the idea. But the prayer this man had prayed, which he went on to describe to me, was quite all right, I thought. In fact I strongly commended it. The substance of his prayer was something like this:

Lord, the first thing I am going to ask You for is good health: give me a strong body. Then give me the ability to think clearly. Give me honest-to-goodness courage, so I can keep going when the going is hard. And give me real confidence. Finally, just let me know that You are with me—that I'm not going it alone. Lord, give me these five things, and I will do the rest myself.

"And did the Lord give you the five things you asked for?"

"He did indeed, but He didn't just hand them out for the asking," my friend said in his racy style which I soon realized was characteristic. But that he did not take his religion flippantly was apparent. "The Lord put me through a wringer several times and I cried 'ouch' more than once. But He let me feel that He was with me, and that made the going a lot easier. He kept His whole part of the bargain. You can count on God; He won't let you down if you hold Him up."

The man had the makings of a real spiritual philosopher, you might say. But first of all he was a practical man.

"As I practiced what you call spiritual laws I found they worked, just like you said; and I'm not the kind of guy who goes for anything that won't work. Naturally you must have the know-how and keep working at it."

"And you really believe that God's presence is a fact?" I asked again.

"I sure do. I felt it. I still feel it. Don't ask me how I feel it. Just take it from me. I know He is right with me. You don't doubt it yourself, do you?" he asked looking at me suspiciously.

We shook hands on it. That he did have this awareness of God's presence was clearly evident. And the sense of Presence which he had practiced until he became proficient had freed him from fear—and not only that, but from some other personality deficiencies as well. It had made him a toughminded optimist.

The practice of a realistic and balanced attitude toward people is another factor that will help you lose your fear of anyone. It is a pathetic fact that more people than you might suppose are afraid of other persons. All the shy, backward and inferiority sufferers are afraid of other individuals.

If you will excuse another personal reference, I will have to admit of a long and painful struggle with a fear of other people. In my boyhood days in small Ohio towns, the local banker was always the leading citizen, the authentic "big shot" so to say. I remember he lived in the biggest house on the main street. His residence sat back among wide lawns and venerable trees. His driveway swept through big impressive gates up to a stately portico. In my early boyhood the pompous banker rode regally behind a spanking pair of matched horses downtown each morning, home to lunch (dinner they called it in those days), to town again, and back for supper. And of course he was the first in town to chug down Main Street in an automobile. It was all very impressive, right down to his big desk which could be seen through the bank window before which there was much bowing and scraping of all and sundry in whom he literally owned shares. This included just about everyone in town.

On Monday mornings I would often accompany my preacher father to the bank where the banker, as treasurer of our church, would pay him his weekly salary. Awestruck I would follow Dad into the great man's office, my heart thumping, hands sweating. It cut deeply into my super-sensitive young nature to hear the banker get off his threadbare witticism: "Well, Brother Peale, do you think your sermon of yesterday justifies your pay?" This always riled me. But my father, mature and urbane, gracefully carried off the weekly joviality. He knew it wasn't ill-meant. But as for me I was afraid of bankers for years.

I was also afraid of the loudly successful student—the kind

with the glib tongue who could always make a terrific impression in class. Even though I knew the stuff I was tense and tongue-tied, heart palpitating when called upon by the teacher. And my choice of words always seemed awkward. I was so embarrassed that even if I knew the answer I stated it so poorly that the effect was anything but outstanding. Accordingly, for years I was awestruck in the presence of anyone who talked liked a scholar. (It's a rather mournful fact that I have heard of practically none of those "bright" students since they left school.)

This wasn't all the pathetic story. I was brought up to think that a politician was of a higher breed, a kind of immortal personality, one with Washington and Lincoln. When the congressman came to town it was quite a day; and if the governor or senator came it was a smashing historical event. I gazed in petrified awe at these "heroic" figures. As for a president or candidate for president—I all but swooned when he passed through our town on the rear end of a train, waving grandly like a conquering Caesar to us country bumpkins.

As I was growing up old Grover B———— was nominated for Congress. Prior to this nobody had ever given old Grover B———— a second thought. But like many small fry he finagled the nomination of the majority party in our area and was elected. The first time I met him after his election I was so awed I could only mumble a few awkward words to this now great figure of history, for, what do you know, he was now actually a Congressman. I can say now that all such adulation has completely passed away. I cite this personal story to illustrate how one can live miserably in abject and shrinking fear of other people.

Essentially my delivery from fear came from learning to use the power of creative thought. Ella Wheeler Wilcox describes very well what right thinking can mean to you:

> Man is what he thinks. Not what he says, reads or
> hears. By persistent thinking you can undo any condi-
> tion which exists. You can free yourself from any chains,
> whether of poverty, sin, ill-health, unhappiness or fear.

There is only one thought pattern that is stronger than
fear, only one that definitely is stronger than fear, and that
is faith. And this does not mean faith in general but faith in
particular. It is faith in God, real and humble faith in God
your Father.

Let me close this chapter with a vignette which illustrates
the kind of faith that can heal a fear condition. I once held in
my hands a Bible said to have been used by Abraham Lincoln
during the Civil War. It was a big rugged-looking Bible: its
appearance much in keeping, I thought, with the character of
Lincoln himself. The Bible fell open to the 34th Psalm, one
verse of which seemed to have been much pondered by Lincoln, for in the margin there was an indented and smudged
place, indicating, it is presumed, that the Emancipator's finger
often rested there at the fourth verse: "I sought the Lord, and
he heard me, and delivered me from all my fears." (Psalm
34:4)

And indeed the Lord will do just that, so don't ever be
afraid of anybody or anything in this life.

THREE

HOW TO HANDLE SITUATIONS
AND YOURSELF WHEN
YOU GET UPSET

No one can expect to go through life without encountering difficulties. No one can live fully and not be upset on occasion. But there are ways of facing up to difficulties and there are techniques that can and should be employed when you are upset. I learned this the hard way, myself, not so long ago. It was a painful experience, but I did learn. That is the important thing.

Let me start, not at the beginning, but at the end. For the end result is the result that counts. The very difficult situation which I faced in the autumn of 1960 forced me back more deeply into prayer and soul searching than ever before in my life. Here and now I would like to share with anyone who is distressed or upset the benefits I gained and the lessons I learned from that experience.

Of one thing I am sure: any soul-wrenching experience brings with it an opportunity to grow. A spiritually mature person will always try to find creative values in even the hardest trials. And so, when this crisis came into my life, I began asking myself how I could use it to deepen my own spiritual awareness and perhaps be more helpful to others who were faced with upsetting situations or problems.

Thinking and praying along this line, the revelation finally came that perhaps I needed a good hard knock and that the Lord wanted to humble me. Everything had gone too well for me: too much success, too many people speaking favorably about me. Perhaps a sharp set-back in life was what I needed to test my belief in certain principles, to try my faith. Anyway, that was exactly what I got. It was one of the most upsetting experiences of my life.

I have written books on positive thinking and emotional and mental control. The principles and teachings of these books have, of course, been my own personal rules for living. I have sincerely practiced them in thought and action over many years. As a result, I found for myself the values I have assured my readers would come to any who think and live on the basis of these positive attitudes.

Forgive me if I plead special circumstances, but this philosophy which I have taught made it all the more difficult for me when I found that I was upset. Actually I was upset because I was upset, for I had come to believe that I had conquered any tendency I may have had of falling into a disturbed mental condition. The startling realization that I could get that way, plus the distress of mind the situation itself had caused me, were very disturbing.

There are many things that can upset a person. Making a foolish mistake can be upsetting. Having your motives questioned or misinterpreted can be upsetting. Being criticized by your colleagues can be upsetting. Facing an unexpected blast of hostility can be upsetting. Getting rattled can be upsetting. Questioning your own intelligence can be upsetting. All these things happened to me, and they all happened at once.

During the early part of the national election campaign of 1960, I was traveling in Europe and the Holy Land. In London, near the end of my trip, I found in my mail an invitation to a meeting of ministers and laymen to be held in Washington, D.C., on September 7, which was the day after my scheduled return to the United States. The meeting was being called to consider the question of separation of church and state.

This, of course, is a question of historic significance, and one that I felt then to be of importance, as I still do. This is a principle for which men have fought, and paid dearly, sometimes with their lives. Acting separately, church and state may complement each other, but when they are one and the same, the true functions of each are distorted. For years I have stressed the relation of religion to the freedom of man on the basis of Jesus' teaching, "Ye shall know the truth, and the truth shall make you free." (John 8:32)

On the very night of my return from Europe, I flew from New York to Washington and, next morning, found myself present at this meeting of about 150 persons. Some of these were old friends, who welcomed me, and I foolishly and thoughtlessly allowed myself to be pressed into service as Chairman of the morning session, even though I then had scant knowledge of the agenda, and had scarcely collected my wits after my travels. After presiding for a short time I left the meeting for quite an extended period, making telephone calls relating to my own personal business. I recall that after finishing the telephone calls I went out to the street and walked up and down the block. It was a fearfully hot day, and I dislike meetings anyway. After about an hour in any meeting I get restless and want to leave. I remember that I hesitated about returning to the session at all and considered passing it up, but, finally, reluctantly returned.

Looking back, I am amazed at my own lack of perceptiveness relative to such a gathering as this, especially at such a time. I was aware, of course, that the political campaign was about to enter the tense, closing months of electioneering. Yet I saw no reason why a group of ministers and laymen should not get together to discuss a topic as important as religious freedom. The meeting proceeded, it seemed to me, in an orderly and reasonable manner. But I should have realized that reporters—ever alert for a big story—were going to pounce on anything that could possibly be related to politics. And I should have realized that, since I acted as chairman, even though for a short time, the meeting might be identified with me.

Indeed, it actually came to be called "The Peale Group." This astonished me, since I had done nothing whatsoever to organize this group, and presided briefly more as an accommodation than anything else.

Those in charge of this meeting prepared a statement for release to newspaper reporters, which contained several important principles. I saw this statement after it had been completed, and had no part at all in its writing. It seemed a temperate and reasoned discussion of some problems that were considered important by many thoughtful people. It asserted a belief in the principle of the separation of church and state. It asserted also a belief that this issue in the political campaign was being suppressed. And let's face it: it *was* an issue in many people's minds. Should any real issue ever be suppressed in a free nation?

Under our American freedom anyone has the right to think for himself and to express his convictions on any subject to the extent of his qualifications. Yet on this issue there had been a kind of public conspiracy of silence. Even to call it an issue was named bigotry. A bigot is defined as one who is obstinately or intolerably devoted to his own church or party or opinion. So, by definition, a bigot is a person whose attitude is the antithesis of freedom through his intolerance and authoritarianism. All right thinking men detest bigotry.

The statement went on to strike a balance by stressing the importance of other issues in the campaign. As far as I could see, it was not at all the intention of this group to allow the religious issue to get out of hand, and this fact was carefully elaborated and stressed. Finally, the statement recommended consideration of the religious issue to each voter's conscience. It did not pretend to answer the question. It merely tried to end an unnatural silence.

I can only say that had I realized all the possible implications of my presence at this conference I would never have attended. I should have realized that any statement of this sort, however temperate, however well-intentioned, in the midst of a political campaign was going to be like a spark in a keg of gunpowder. It was going to cause an explosion. It was going to liberate all the suppressed fury and hostility on both sides. In failing to foresee this, I was naive. And I never was a political thinker.

What hurt the most, I think, after the release of this statement was to find myself actually accused of bigotry; me, accused of bigotry! This is a point on which I am especially sensitive, for all my life I have devoted myself to combatting intolerance. I have worked with organizations trying to eliminate bigotry in national and racial, as well as religious matters. I founded the largest inter-faith publication in our country. I have made it a special point to try to develop harmony among the leading religious groups in the United States—the Jews, the Catholics, and the Protestants. When you have worked all your life to reduce bigotry, it is quite upsetting to be castigated as guilty of the very thing you have labored diligently to eliminate.

I found that this Washington meeting was a milestone in my own personal life and, in retrospect, I realize that it also was a milestone in the history of free religious thought and discussion in America. From my harrowing experience it became crystal clear that it is no longer possible in this country to discuss the great principle of religious freedom, however dispassionately and objectively. As far as I am personally concerned I shall never again be involved in any consideration of religious freedom whatsoever, for I realize that to do so is to court the danger of being accused of bigotry. Though I love religious freedom, I hate bigotry more.

I want no sympathy, but I will tell you that as I walked the streets of Washington after the storm broke on the day following the meeting, I was appalled at finding myself actually trying to avoid the glances of passers-by for fear I should encounter one of my many Roman Catholic friends who might mistakenly think I had turned against him. I was in acute distress at the unbelievable turn events had taken, sick at heart with irritation at my own ineptness.

In an effort to dispel the erroneous impression that I had been a leader, or *the* leader, of the group, I notified those in charge that I would no longer be associated in any way with it. Then I retired to my farm in the country, shutting myself off completely from newspapers and television, whose representatives clamored for "statements."

But even this was a mistake. I should have faced the press and told the story as frankly and calmly as I am telling it now. The truth is, I was so upset that I doubted my ability to make myself clear or to convey my actual feelings. I dreaded any more misrepresentation, or over-simplification. It is thus that one small mistake can lead to another, and another, and another. The more mistakes we make, the more rattled we get, and the more mistakes we make. I was also distressed by the sharp and I thought quite eager personal attacks on me that came from two eminent, though politically conditioned theological professors, who loudly castigated me as head of the "Protestant underworld," whatever that is, and called me a bigot. I made no reply. Again, however, this policy of silence proved unwise, in that it allowed false material to build up and to gain wide circulation.

This chapter, despite several pages being devoted to the Washington meeting, is not intended either as an explanation or as a defense of my participation. The rather lengthy recital of this incident is primarily for the purpose of showing how one person, myself in this instance, could become involved in and have to deal with a most upsetting experience.

This chapter is essentially designed to be a sort of laboratory of discovered and demonstrated methods for handling yourself and situations when you get upset. In short, we are presenting here no theoretical problem, but an actual and very difficult personal experience as a testing ground for the workable techniques outlined for your possible use.

I can assure you that I know for a fact that the methods described in this chapter will work, since they worked for me in about as tough a situation as anyone could get into. My experience as a laboratory experiment in dealing with upsetness may possibly be helpful to others in their own difficulties.

The extent of my upset state of mind is indicated by the fact that I cancelled all of my scheduled speaking engagements for fear that my presence on a program might possibly embarrass my sponsors. Of forty engagements, thirty-eight vigorously rejected my withdrawal, and they were secular meetings in which were represented people of all religious faiths.

So deeply into my consciousness did my upsetting reactions penetrate that I resigned the pastorate of my church where I had served for twenty-eight years. No one had suggested or even hinted at such an action, but as the furor around me mounted and criticisms came from Jewish, Catholic and Protestant sources, the thought came and would not down that I had, God help me, brought disrepute on the church and people I loved. I developed the feeling that I must be an embarrassment to my church and congregation and therefore must remove myself from my pastorate.

Accordingly I submitted my resignation to my Elders and Deacons, an action which seemed to be received with considerable surprise. It was immediately and unanimously rejected. Of course, I was deeply moved by this expression of confidence by my brethren. Their assurances of brotherliness and prayer greatly strengthened me.

I wrote a letter to the members of our congregation with all of whom I have always been on terms of Christian affection and true spiritual understanding. It means much when in difficulty for you to have the friendship and spiritual support of those who know you best. This understanding and love between spiritual friends is surely one of the greatest blessings of life, especially in times of crisis. I had been privileged as a pastor to help them; now how kind they were in being of help to me. This truly is bearing one another's burdens.

In order that you, my reader, may enter more completely into the feeling between the congregation and myself, I am printing here the letter to our members, even though it does contain some references already made in this chapter.

September 15, 1960

Dear Friends:

As a member of Marble Collegiate Church and one who has always given your pastor sincere and prayerful support in his work, I feel that I want to enlighten you first-hand on recent events.

I refer to a widely publicized meeting of ministers held in Washington on September 7, 1960. This is being called in the press "the Peale group," which of course is entirely inaccurate, therefore I would like to give you the exact facts.

While in Europe I received an invitation to attend a Study Conference on Religion and Freedom scheduled for Washington on September 7. Beyond the names of a few people who were to be present, I had no information on the meeting itself, but I had respect for those whose names were given to me.

I arrived in New York from Europe on the afternoon of September 6, and therefore had no opportunity to secure further information on the meeting. Had I not agreed to attend a Spiritual Retreat of another group, which included some of our own church members, on September 8 in Washington, I probably would not have attended the September 7 Religion and Freedom meeting.

In Washington I was asked to preside, which I did in the morning session only. I left at the conclusion of the afternoon session and have had no further contact with this group.

To give you full information relative to my part in this affair, may I say the following:

1. I did not call the meeting or have any part in calling it.

2. I had no part whatever in preparing the statement issued by the group.

3. Upon returning to New York, I sent the Executive Secretary a telegram stating that I would not further be associated with their program in any way.

Despite this fact, the press has continued to call this "the Peale group" or "a group headed by Dr. Peale." I am not the head of the group and have never been such, and it is not "the Peale group." In fact, I do not now or never have had any relationship with the group, except attendance upon this one meeting.

I felt a sense of concern about the matter of religious freedom and believe it is proper at any time for a Protestant to meet with fellow Protestants to discuss matters relating to our faith. It is the American right to assemble and to consider, and in this instance it was done with dignity and with a view towards lifting the religious discussion towards a higher intellectual level and to divest it of heat and emotionalism.

I might have known, and I am amazed that I did not realize that under the circumstances this would immediately get involved in the political campaign. I sincerely did not mean it to be so, but perhaps I will be a wiser person in the future—at least, let us hope so.

I was so distressed by the inadvertent injection of myself into political publicity, which actually is contrary to my own nature, that I completely isolated myself from the press for fear I would only make matters worse by anything I might say. As a result, the press has continued to emphasize me personally, without reference to any of the 150 persons present, which I must say seems unfair.

Always being sensitive about our beloved Church, I felt that this unhappy situation might bring disrepute upon it, so I offered my resignation to our Elders and Deacons. They held a meeting and refused to consider the resignation. My heart was touched by the realization that my brethren had sufficient confidence in my true spirit to realize that this situation was not representative of my humble ministry.

For many years I have worked in the inter-faith field and sincerely trust that I may continue to do so, despite all that has been said. I am going to find it a bit difficult perhaps to carry on, and will need your prayers, and hope I may be worthy of your support. I do not feel that I was wrong in attending this meeting, but it may have been unwise under the circumstances. There are certain spiritual principles which we Protestants hold, but we are certainly not against any other faith, for that matter, and we should cultivate only love and brotherhood in our hearts.

It is difficult for me to write you this letter, and I trust

you will pray most earnestly for our Church, and perhaps for me.

Yours in Christian fellowship,
(Signed) Norman Vincent Peale

After that grim time in Washington and the painful days
that followed, when the Sunday came for me to return to
the Marble Collegiate Church in New York, I was hardly
prepared for the expression of love and support which I experienced. When I walked into the pulpit the capacity congregation rose silently en masse, something I had never before
witnessed in my lifetime in church. This surprise standing of
the congregation and the expression on the faces of the people
made me choke up. I motioned to them to be seated, but felt
a surge of strength and a new dedication within me.

Now, as I say, there would be little point in recalling this
whole experience of mine unless I learned something from it—
something worth passing along to others. And I honestly believe that I did. Though I admit that I floundered badly at
times, nevertheless, I began to evolve a technique (because
it's composed of formulas that work) for handling oneself and
situations when upset.

With this technique I gradually pulled back, with God's
help, to a normal state of mind. Let me describe the method
I found helpful, as I am sure it can help you too.

From my own upsetting experience I learned that a first
step is carefully and honestly to analyze the entire situation,
and your own actions, and if you feel that you acted unwisely,
simply come right out and admit it. The most important result
of this is that it enables you to deal realistically with the situation from this point. Instead of self-justification and rational-
ization to blur your judgment, you gain a true perspective and
this, at least, puts an end to the pyramiding mistakes.

Another value of this first step is that it is a highly effective
answer to critics. If you agree with them, what more can they

say? By your agreement you have stolen their thunder. The mistake is thus mitigated, for who isn't unwise, even stupid, at some time or other? We all make mistakes. The late Fiorello LaGuardia, Mayor of New York City, was completely forgiven, and never more loved, than when he said (as I have heard him quoted), "I don't make mistakes very often, but when I do make one, it's a beaut!" What that mistake was, no one now remembers, but his apology for it is probably immortal.

The truth is, if you feel you have made a mistake and can summon up the courage to say so, people will rally to your support in a way that is heartening and astonishing.

A second step to take when you're upset is to make yourself become deliberately analytical and objective. This will tend quickly to extract the heat of emotional reaction from your mind and, as mental heat cools off, normal attitudes and clear thinking again become possible. For example, in considering any unkind things that may have been said about you, the scientific objective approach consists in asking four questions: (1) Is it true or false? (2) Who said it? (3) Is his opinion of any value? (4) Is he an honest or a prejudiced critic?

In my case, take the assertion by a theological professor who is also a politician, vice-chairman of a political party, that I am of the "Protestant Underworld." Frankly, this could be upsetting—and was. But I asked myself, "Is what this man says true?" Of course, it wasn't. Therefore, I reminded myself of the expression, "Saying doesn't make it so." No matter what this man said, as long as it was not true, why should I be concerned about it? I recalled an old proverb in which I have often taken comfort, "A lie cannot run very far for it has short legs."

A man once came to me who was very upset by remarks made by a former friend who was now full of hate and anger. "Do you know what that guy does?" he demanded. "He goes around calling me a skunk, a dirty skunk! What do you think of that—a skunk?"

"Well, are you?" I asked him dryly.

"Of course I'm not," he roared. "Do I look like a skunk to you?"

"Certainly you don't. I know you are not a skunk. You know you are not a skunk. So this man's saying so is a falsehood. The mere fact that he says it cannot change a falsehood into truth. So just let him say it. In time people may get a pretty accurate idea of who the skunk really is."

So I learned the hard way to ask myself, "Is what they say true or false?" If true, then, of course, you should be honest and admit it and correct it. But if it isn't true, just remember this—all the saying in the world cannot make a thing true that isn't true. It can give you a lot of trouble and annoyance, but it cannot change the basic facts. And it is still a fact that "truth crushed to earth shall rise again."

A second consideration in this objective-scientific upset-reducing process is to ask, "Who says it?" Is he someone whose opinion you respect? Is he an honest critic, or has he "some fish to fry?" Has he some purpose of his own that will be served by trying to depreciate you? An honest critic is to be respected if he is not personal or vicious; but as to the other kind, simply write him off. What he says is of no importance.

Still another element in the process of siphoning off the emotional content of an upsetting situation, a further application of the objective-scientific method, is to take apart quite dispassionately remarks that are designed to upset you and carefully study their implications. I laid that epithet, "Protestant Underworld," out on the laboratory table and meticulously examined it. "Underworld," of course, connotes gangsters, crooks, thugs, hi-jackers, murderers and other unsavory characters. This description of some Protestants seemed more severe than the facts indicated. While I have known some

Protestants who could scarcely qualify as saints, I could not recall any who rated such an uncomplimentary reference as "underworld."

Therefore, I concluded that the term "Protestant underworld" was unspecific and ill-chosen; that actually it did not apply, since it referred to a non-existent supposition. How could I head or even be a member of something that did not exist? The result of such dispassionate and objective analytical reasoning was to pull the sting of the criticism and render it impotent to hurt me. I simply wrote it off as a rather silly effort to coin a phrase and gain publicity with it. But since it had no substance in fact, it was ineffective, except for its smear value.

It was thus that I dealt with my own upset feelings over the remarks of a few political theologians who deplore "politics" on the part of any minister who disagrees with them, but who regard it a pious and praiseworthy activity when they themselves become party politicians.

This wasn't enough, of course, for one must become positive and try to have no personal ill will toward people. This further step I believe to be vital to a permanent victory over an upset mental state. Having good will does not necessarily mean affection, but rather a cool esteem for the ego or personality of the other person, even if you do not respect his judgment and actions. That feeling I was able to achieve.

The objective-scientific method works out in many ways. Suppose someone has taken some hostile action against you or in some other way has done something to hurt you. Suppose this someone is a former friend. It is important to realize that friends can often upset us even more than enemies, for it is a psychological truth that those who love the most can hurt the most. If, therefore, you are upset because of something a friend has done or said, the objective-scientific method is to analyze the issue coolly and calmly on the basis of the deeply intertwined love-hate reaction. If the friend seems now even to hate you, it very well could be that his so-called hate is actually the reverse side of a wounded love he holds for you. So just keep on esteeming him and slant your mind away from his present words and deeds by saying, "He doesn't really mean it the way it sounds and appears, and I shall not take it as such."

This attitude must be accompanied by a careful analysis of what caused the other person to react as he has toward you. Look into yourself to identify and appraise the reasons you rub him the wrong way. Practice the empathy technique, which is to project your mind into the other person's mind and think from there. See and think as he sees and thinks. See yourself as he sees you and then carefully consider your own actions from his point of view. It is very possible, of course, that he is wrong about you, but when you know why he is wrong, how he made that mistake, it is easier to correct whatever in you gives him that erroneous impression. This process can also clearly reveal to you your weak points as others view them. It will afford you the chance to improve yourself personally and your performance generally.

The objective-scientific method has still another use that is very effective in reducing upset feelings regarding a hurtful action against you. Simply ask yourself, "Did this person have the right to do what he did? Was he acting in accordance with the requirements of his job as he sees them?" If he had the right to do as he did and was only doing what he felt the situation required, he certainly is not open to condemnation. You may not like what he did and regret it, but objectively your disagreement with his action justifies no hostility or even hurt on your part. This rational mental approach has a definite cooling effect on your own heated upset feelings. Think it through. See the other fellow's viewpoint and in a friendly attitude accept his perfect right to have done what he did about you.

I can assure you that this procedure is most effective in handling yourself and situations when you are upset, for it proved so in my painful experience. I make no claims to perfection. However, I have often used this method in personal relationships and the result has been uniformly good. It has helped me to keep my emotions under control and it has had thereby a beneficial effect on personal relations.

Naturally, it hasn't made everything turn out my way. Why should everything go my way or your way? We have to have some strike-outs in the game of life. But maybe, just maybe, those who strike out the oftenest are those who try the hardest to hit the ball. Babe Ruth was the greatest home run hitter of all time, but he also had one of the largest number of strike-outs. This proves that he tried to hit. He went after some pitches and missed them, in fact, he missed a lot of them, but the average number that he did hit made him a champion. At least, he reached for them. He tried and he didn't get discouraged by failure and stop trying. If he had he wouldn't have been Babe Ruth.

So I do not claim that the philosophy and formula for action which I advocate will cause everything to go well. You will get some reverses and disappointments, even with this method, but the fact remains that you won't be nearly so upset and that is the problem we are working on in this chapter.

If you don't mind another personal illustration of my own struggles with being upset, I would like to tell you how I used the rational questioning process, "Does he have the right to do this to me? Is he acting in accordance with the requirements of his job?" This sort of questioning really helped in my case.

When the furor broke about my attendance at the Washington meeting, two of the newspapers for which I write a weekly column became disturbed. They cancelled my column forthwith and announced the fact in front page notices. This column appears weekly in approximately two hundred newspapers, some large, some small.

The two papers that cancelled immediately were in large Eastern cities and were outlets that I greatly regretted losing. I must admit that this incident added to my distress of mind. I received many letters condemning these publishers on the ground that they acted precipitously without knowing all the facts, that they were denying the right of free speech, of a man to be a citizen as well as a writer. Others compared these two papers unfavorably with the 198 other papers which took the matter calmly, who insisted on the right of a man to think and speak his convictions, or who simply had confidence in me to the extent of letting me make one mistake, even though a bad one.

But although I appreciated the efforts of my well-meaning defenders, I decided to apply the "Has he the right?" formula.

The publisher of one of these papers was a friend of mine over quite a few years. I had been with him and his family on various occasions and felt a personal bond with him. I admired him as a man and as a constructive citizen. He and I were, I felt, on the same "team," working for human welfare.

Therefore when he dropped my column from his newspaper in which it had appeared for a number of years, I was not only deeply disappointed, but maybe a little hurt at this action by a friend. So it was necessary to go to work on my spirit regarding his action. I asked myself, "Has he the right to do this?" And naturally the answer was—of course he had. It's a free country and it's his paper and he has the right to determine what does and does not go into his own publications.

Still using the scientific-objective-dispassionate mental process, I then asked, "Is he acting in accordance with the requirements of his job?" And again, I had to admit that he was the sole judge of the policy of his paper and was entitled to respect for his decisions. By this process of thinking, therefore, I satisfied my mind that he had simply come to the point where he sincerely felt that my contribution was no longer of value to his paper, and that, as they say, was that.

Now should this change my opinion of him as a person, or be any reason for altering my friendly attitude toward him? Not at all! If the publishing of my column depends only upon a friendly feeling on the part of an editor, rather than upon its merit, it is not a substantial basis for its inclusion. An editor may actually dislike my column and disagree with my words and actions and still be a friend on a personal basis. And the same is true of my feeling for an editor. I found it helpful in curbing upset feelings to make the distinction between personal disappointment, which is an emotional response, and the recognized right of an editor to run his own business, which is an objective consideration.

I therefore wrote to the editors of both papers which cancelled, thanking them for the privilege which had been mine of contribution to their newspapers for so long a time. I also explained as clearly as I could my part in the Washington affair. One then wrote me the following kindly letter:

September 28, 1960

Dear Dr. Peale:

Thank you very much for your sympathetic and understanding letter. Under the circumstances, cancellation of your column seemed the only thing to do due to the great number of letters and telephone calls received after the Washington meeting, and inasmuch as the wire stories implied political overtones. The right or wrong in such matters is scarcely ever discovered until it is too late. I'm sure you understand that an editor must be sensitive to public reaction—at least what appears to be reader protest.

However, you will be glad to learn that the tide has turned and that you have many more admirers among our half million subscribers than I realized. Perhaps I acted in haste, but I did what I then believed was right.

This will be easy for you to understand as you have just experienced the unfortunate result of second-guessing yourself. I suspect, though, that as a clergyman, your hindsight is not quite as painful as that of a newspaper editor. And it was nice to know that your congregation didn't take the same dim view of your plight as I, a condition in which you have my sincere congratulations and best wishes.

Sincerely yours,

So an important technique for dealing with your upset feelings and with upsetting situations, is the application of the objective-scientific method in which finally you become dispassionate in attitude. Dispassionate means, of course, to be without passion. It implies the ability to employ reason and maintain emotional control whatever the provocation.

Practice reason always. Make use of that most uncommon quality known as common sense. Into the nervous, jittery, darkling condition of your depressed mind, drive the long light of common sense, or pure unadulterated reason. Simply ask yourself how much sense it makes getting upset. Where, frankly, will it get you? What good can it possibly do for you to get in a stew and remain agitated, disturbed, depressed, even angry. Give yourself the coldly rationalistic treatment. Ask yourself, "How much and for how long shall I go on hurting myself? Frankly, am I deliberately trying to destroy myself? Am I feasting on the bitter-sweet of self pity?" These and other searching questions should be pondered and dealt with.

Obviously it is difficult to employ reason and common sense in a situation which is highly charged with emotion and hurt, resentment and self-pity. Self-discipline is required. But what is wrong with self-discipline? The mere fact that a soft generation isn't trained in this manly art does not reflect upon self-discipline, but rather upon us who do not practice it because "it's too hard."

Plato said, and it's a remark that can revolutionize you, "Take charge of your life. You can do what you will with it." Ask yourself in no uncertain terms, "Just where will being upset get me except to further upset me?" If you remain upset long enough, you will be through as far as meeting life effectively is concerned. And it will be you who will have finished you—no one else. You simply cannot blame other people and situations for doing to you what actually you do to yourself if you acquiesce with and settle down into a permanently upset mental state.

I recognize, of course, that this advice is more easily given than practiced. It is more easily said than done. I had a hard time practicing it myself. But while it is not an easy course to follow, neither is it an impossible one. I have been charged with advocating "easy religion" by people who misunderstand or are not familiar with my teachings. No one can amount to anything in this tough world unless he is somewhat of a man. Such self-discipline as is demanded in the formula outlined in this chapter is rugged. To accomplish it, you need help, real help, the kind of help that only God can supply. Throughout this book we suggest how that help may be had.

One thing you and I must learn is that most of the trouble with life is within ourselves, but fortunately the solution also is to be found within us. So draw more deeply upon the power of life which is within you. This solution called The Kingdom of God is a powerful recreative force deep down in your personality waiting to be summoned forth. When you do summon it and put it to work in your life you will live with so much power that nothing can really upset you again, at least not to the point of defeating you.

Sum-up of *How To Handle Yourself and Situations When You Get Upset*

1. Analyze the situation carefully and determine if you acted unwisely. Admit all your mistakes openly and honestly, telling the whole truth and admitting your ineptness.

2. Utilize the scientific-objective approach to mean or unkind things said about you, asking yourself: Is it true or false? Who said it? Is his opinion of any value? Is he a prejudiced or honest critic?

3. Apply cool scientific scrutiny to any epithets used against you, taking them apart in a detailed examination to see if they apply. If they do, correct yourself. If they don't, forget it.

4. Keep on esteeming people even when they act badly toward you.

5. Ask another dispassionate question. Did this person have the right to take the action he did? If so, accept it in good faith.

6. Seek the counsel and guidance of thoughtful friends and practice all the cool reason and common sense of which you are capable. Hard as it may be, you must think; you must use reason, not emotion. Any turmoil will ultimately settle down if you do that. And you will get answers that answer.

7. Ask yourself, "Am I enjoying my misery?" Cast off all self-pity.

8. Try loving everyone involved and pray for them, hard as that may be. Loving doesn't mean sentimentality but rather a rational esteem for them as persons.

9. Put the problem in God's hands; let go and let God take it over. He will bring it out better than you think.

———

FOUR

LIKE YOURSELF—AT LEAST
MOST OF THE TIME

He had no idea what was to be thrown at him when he opened the door. And he was anything but prepared. But, even so, he handled the matter satisfactorily although emergency help was required. This young pastor and his even younger bride had moved into the country parsonage only three days before. It was a tiny town and his was a small, white-frame church with modest parsonage next door. The young couple was just sitting down to dinner when the door bell rang.

The caller, a man apparently about thirty-five years old, gave a typically Madison Avenueish and country-clubbish impression. His tailor obviously knew how to ease a man expertly into a suit of clothes that fit like the paper on the wall. Broad shouldered and narrow waisted he was what you might term super-duper Ivy League. He had the sophisticated flair that would, no doubt, make him a knock-out at a cocktail party. A rakish foreign-model sports car was drawn up at the curb.

"You don't know me," he said, "I live in _____ (naming a city not too far away), but I'm in trouble, real trouble." His

68

drawn face underscored the point. "I've been driving around in circles for hours and I'm dead tired."

The pastor invited him in and offered him a chair. Then the visitor continued, "I've got to talk to someone who understands, who is one-hundred per cent confidential. I'm washed up, completely licked; there's no hope, no way out that I can figure. In fact I might as well tell you that you're my last stop. If you can't help me, I'm going to knock myself off if I can muster up the guts."

That he meant what he said was obvious even to the unpracticed young pastor. "How did you happen to come here?" he asked sparring for time to decide on a course of action.

"I've been just driving around, been doing it for I don't know how long, and then I happened to see the church. I don't know why I stopped except maybe—well I was literally raised in Sunday School and church as a boy. Anyway I just felt like stopping."

"What's bothering you?" the young pastor asked.

"I don't know actually. . . . I'm terribly depressed. I hate myself. In fact I'm so d___ sick of myself that I don't want to see myself anymore. What in the h___ can you do for me, Reverend?"

Well, one thing was sure. The Reverend didn't know what he could do. Meanwhile dinner was getting cold but the young wife was philosophical; she put her husband's meal back in the oven, and ate her own.

"Tell you what," said the Reverend. "You sit here and relax for a few minutes." He called to his wife, "Honey, please bring in a cup of hot coffee for our friend here."

"Drink that coffee, it will do you good. And while you're doing that, I've got a short consultation in the back room. I'll be with you soon."

In the back room he stood looking, but not seeing, out the window. He was a real man, college athlete, and a popular leader type. He had been attracted to the ministry initially because a university lecturer had transmitted "a profound concern for the world" to him. Next thing he knew he was in the Theological Seminary trying to find himself, but basically he only got more confused. He was still finding himself and this self he was hunting was elusive.

Minister though he was, he fell into the vernacular: "This sure is a hot one. Gosh, I haven't even made a start on this job and here comes this guy throwing a problem like this at me. And what in the heck do I know about it?"

He quickly raced his mind over his courses in the seminary, desperately trying to pick up a practical idea that might be usable in a personal crisis like this one. "Nothing but philosophy, sociology, social action. That stuff may be O.K. but it's no good here, that's for sure. What's the matter with those professors that they didn't tell me how to understand and help just one human being? What good is all this heavy 'social concern' stuff if I can't help one poor guy! Why don't they get out of their classrooms and get wised up on the facts of life? Gee, I'm a total loss. I haven't got an idea in my head," he moaned.

Then he went into that "consultation." He prayed and even his prayer was down-to-earth. "Lord, I'm stumped. Please tell me what to tell this fellow. Amen."

That is the kind of prayer the Lord likes, if you ask me. It was a succinct statement of real need offered with humility and honest faith. And the Lord did indeed tell him what to tell "the fellow" and how to tell it to him effectively too. Even though he didn't know very much, the pastor did genuinely like human beings and that, of course, is basic in the process of helping others.

From his back room prayer consultation the pastor got the distinct guidance that he should sit down with the man and get him talking. He was also to realize that what the self-disliking fellow needed was for someone to show genuine interest and concern and even more to transmit esteem; to restore faith in his faltering ego. And finally he was to build up the man's hope and make him know for a fact that God would help him. He was to try to bring God into the man's mind as a real factor.

Accordingly he returned to the living room draping his long form over a chair in an easy going, relaxed attitude as though he had all the time in the world. His manner seemed to relieve his visitor's tension to some degree and the latter started talking, haltingly at first; then he really got into it, listing conflicts, moral failures and dishonesties that could indeed undermine self-esteem. The pastor listened with friendly interest, meanwhile deliberately sending out to the other thoughts of esteem. He practiced Frank Laubach's technique of quietly "shooting prayers" toward his visitor. What was the man's problem? One of the most complicated of all in which self-esteem or ego respect had been shattered by successive violations of basic ethical ideas with which he had tried to part company, but couldn't.

After an hour of this the minister stretched himself. "I'm hungry as a bear. You must be starved yourself."

"Honey," he called to his wife, "do you suppose you could rescue a couple of starving guys?"

"Sure thing," she replied from the kitchen, "coming right up."

A short time later the two men were stowing it away, especially the visitor, who evidenced his mental relief by the reassertion of physical hunger. The two men actually joked and kidded a bit and before the meal was over they were calling each other by their first names, Sam for the visitor and Chuck for the pastor.

It was eleven p.m. when Sam and Chuck stood outside by the rakish foreign sports car. "Sam, before you go I'd like to say just one thing more. You're feeling better right now because you have found a friend with whom you could share your trouble and you feel some genuine human support. But Sam that isn't enough. We have got to make a transference from me, a human friend, to that other Friend who can be with you at all times and guide you to the new life you are headed toward."

"I get you, Chuck, and I'd like that."

So the two had a prayer standing there in the silvery moonlight. Just a short prayer. Chuck prayed, "Lord take over with Sam and go with him. Help him really to let You run his life." Then he said, "Now you pray, Sam."

"You mean out loud? I never did that in my life."

"I know and now is the time to start; besides, we're friends aren't we?"

After a long hesitation Sam said, "Dear Lord, thanks for Chuck. You surely led me to him. I need You. Please take over and run my life. Please help me. Amen."

After Sam had disappeared down the highway gunning his car, Chuck walked up and down in front of his little church with an elation he had never felt. Tears welled up in his eyes. Suddenly he loved the whole world and especially the tiny church gleaming white in the moonlight.

"Gosh," he said aloud, "I wouldn't have missed being a minister for anything. Thank you, God, for bringing Sam to me. I'll stick with him until he really finds You and then he and I will help others all down the years."

With two jumps he was in the house where he surprised his wife by swinging her off her feet and dancing around the room with her. "Stop, stop," she cried. "I'm out of breath. Whatever has got into you?"

"Boy, it's wonderful, simply wonderful, this ministry. Honey, God was in this house tonight."

She stopped before him. "Let me look at you, Chuck dear.

I never before saw that look on your face. It is simply wonderful. You are positively exalted." Then very tenderly: "I've got a new insight into you. My Chuck is really a man of—God." That night Chuck became a tough-minded optimist.

This first case of Chuck's, as he set up as a spiritual practitioner, had to do with a man who had developed an extreme dislike for himself, an abnormal self-hatred brought on by wrong thinking and living. In the process of spiritual change which eventually brought vital new life to Sam, Chuck evolved a formula or you might even say a prescription that proved helpful to many. It was: (1) Learn really to know yourself. (2) Learn really to esteem yourself. (3) Learn really to let God run your life.

This chapter on liking yourself may seem a bit bewildering, at least most of the time. You may perhaps think of persons whose egos are seemingly anything but underdeveloped, who apparently like themselves very much indeed. It would seem quite unnecessary to stimulate a further liking of themselves. But it is not super self-love or inflated admiration of the ego that we would encourage, but rather plain, normal self-esteem—this being a mark of balanced personality.

That bumptious self-assurance, commonly referred to as egotism, is more often than not a cover-up for a sense of inferiority and self-dislike. The offensively egotistical are often the most unsure. Egotism is a protective device of the personality to shore up its lack of faith in itself. It is a dubious method by which the personality seeks to cover up a state of unhappiness with oneself.

Not liking oneself is a widespread problem of human beings and accounts for much of the hurt we inflict upon ourselves and other people.

William Nichols, Editor of *This Week* Magazine, has published some of his choice "Words to Live By" pieces in a delightful book bearing that title. One by John Steinbeck describes a man who suffered from self-dislike:

> "For a very long time I didn't like myself . . . for a number of reasons, some of them valid and some of them pure fancy.
>
> "Then gradually," he said, "I discovered with surprise and pleasure that a number of people did like me. And I thought, If they can like me, why can't I like myself? Slowly I learned to like myself and then it was all right."
>
> . . . He meant literally that he had learned to accept and like the person Ed as he liked other people. . . . Most people do not like themselves at all.
>
> Once Ed was able to like himself he was released from the secret prison of self-contempt.*

Maxwell Maltz, M.D. shows how our image of ourself determines our liking ourself:

> The self-image we harbor is the key to the success or failure of our most cherished plans and aspirations. If the image is inadequate—and psychologists say most of us habitually underrate ourselves—it behooves us to correct it. We do this by systematically imagining that we are already the sort of person we wish to be. If you have been painfully shy, imagine yourself moving among people with ease and poise. If you have been fearful and over-anxious, see yourself acting calmly, confidently and with courage.
>
> If we picture ourselves performing in a certain manner, this imaginative exercise impresses our subconscious almost as much as does actual performance.
>
> *Dehypnotize Yourself.* What we believe about ourselves often imposes rigid and quite false limits on what we are able to accomplish. As a schoolboy Dr. Alfred Adler, the famous psychiatrist, got off to a bad start in

---

* "Liking Yourself" by John Steinbeck, pp. 10–11, *Words to Live By*, edited by William Nichols, Simon and Schuster, © 1959.

arithmetic. His teacher became convinced that he was "dumb in mathematics." Adler passively accepted the evaluation, and his grades seemed to prove it correct. One day, however, he had a sudden flash of insight and announced that he thought he could solve a problem the teacher had put on the board which none of the other pupils could work. The whole class laughed. Whereupon he became indignant, strode to the blackboard and worked the problem. In doing so, he realized that he could understand arithmetic. He felt a new confidence in his ability, and went on to become a good math student.

The point is this: Adler had been hypnotized by a false belief about himself. Not figuratively but literally and actually hypnotized. For the power of hypnosis *is* the power of belief. If you have accepted an idea—from yourself, your teachers, parents, friends or any other source—and if you are convinced that idea is true, it has the same power over you as the hypnotist's words have over his subject.

Negative thinking can limit each of us if we let it. And, conversely, within you right now is the power to do things you never dreamed possible.*

And of course when you know and appreciate and use your powers, your knowledge of yourself grows into self-esteem and, as a result, your liking for yourself increases.

Self-dislike carried to the extreme often results in mental or nervous breakdown and other forms of retreat from reality. Reason may even be dethroned if self-dislike becomes sufficiently intense. A physician declared: "Asylums are filled with people who dislike, even hate themselves. Many retreated from life to escape themselves."

* "Your Built-In 'Success Mechanism,'" condensed from *Psycho-Cybernetics* by Maxwell Maltz, M.D. (Prentice-Hall, Inc., 1960), pp. 222–224, *Reader's Digest*, April 1961.

In less aggravated form people dislike their looks, wishing they were taller, shorter, heavier or thinner. They have very little confidence in themselves, being shy, shrinking and self-doubting. Plagued by persistent inner conflict, which always siphons off energy, they literally get tired deep within themselves and so they literally get tired of themselves. Often inept and blundering, doing awkward even stupid things, they become exasperated, not with other people, but with their own personalities. They get on their own nerves, you might say. They have no fun with themselves. They are bored by themselves and fed up with what they think they are. Dr. Maltz further says:

> Each of us has a mental picture of himself, a self-image which governs much of his conduct and outlook. To find life reasonably satisfying you must have a self-image that you can live with. You must find yourself acceptable to you. You must have a self that you like, and one that you can trust and believe in. When this self-image is one you can be proud of, you feel self-confident. You function at your best.*

Whenever I consider this self-dislike problem of human nature, I always recall the harassed and unhappy man who fumed, "I would give a half-year's salary (and that was a pretty figure, too) if only I could enjoy a two-weeks' vacation from myself." But of course this is not possible. You are forever tied to yourself. It is well named, *your*self. It's *yours* for keeps. There is no escape, no alternative, no out. You have to live with yourself every minute of every day and night as long as you are alive. You can never get away from yourself, from that three-part entity of body, mind and soul called "you." Maybe it's a hard, unpleasant fact but that's the way it is—you're stuck with yourself.

* Ibid., pp. 217–218.

This being an inescapable fact, it is only sensible to figure out how to live with yourself in some sort of peace and happiness at *least* most of the time. That qualifying phrase, "at least most of the time," is intended to acknowledge the realistic fact that even in the normal, balanced personality there is still resident within human nature a vague and haunting dissatisfaction. In the well-integrated individual this is not persistent and certainly not dominant, but there will be moments, or perhaps only fractions of moments, when self-dissatisfaction will manifest itself. It cannot be avoided. Some of this restlessness is probably always going to be present within you.

Perhaps, as a matter of fact, this dissatisfaction factor may be a basic mechanism installed in human nature by the Creator to act as insurance against our becoming too smugly content with ourselves. And a certain amount of discontent, annoying though it may be, is important to that continued drive or motivation without which progress toward goals would not be possible. So the qualifying phrase "most of the time" acknowledges the inherent fact that a certain amount of discontent with yourself adds balance to your personality, development, and increases your assurance of success in life. No smugly satisfied person ever gets very far, or having gotten there stays there.

How, then, can you learn to like yourself? Simply learn to know yourself. You may not like someone but when you come to know that person, as your knowledge of him grows you find yourself liking him. It is a fact that much dislike of other people is based upon inadequate and therefore inconclusive knowledge of them.

The same law of human nature applies to your relation with yourself. As you learn really to know your own self you will discover depth qualities you never knew you possessed. You will find that you are more likeable than you thought and so your opinion of yourself will improve until finally you will actually enjoy living with yourself.

And it is of practical value to learn to like yourself. Since you must spend so much time with yourself you might as well get some satisfaction out of the relationship. There's little sense living unhappily with yourself or being on the outs with your own personality, especially since it is not necessary to do so. Therefore it's only smart to get on good terms with yourself.

To do this make an honest and thorough self-analysis: doing a comprehensive size-up job on yourself. See and study your best self aspects. Then form a mental picture of your best and most likeable self. Think in terms of that self, getting that picture clearly defined in your mind. Hold the thought image persistently, firmly imbedding it in your consciousness. See or visualize it as emerging into a dominant position of control in your personality. If you will believe this formula and practice it your best-self concept will become you in fact. For with your entire consciousness supporting your mental picture it tends to actualize itself.

Remember those significant words of the sage Marcus Aurelius—"The soul is dyed the color of its thoughts." He is telling you that within your thinking process you can select the life coloration which you desire and bring it to actualization by the type of thoughts you use habitually. There is an old oriental maxim which says, "What you think upon, grows." You can think yourself into being the attractive self you want to be.

But there is something deeper involved here than trying to like yourself by mentally picturing your best and most likeable self. I must warn you that your worse self is a pretty bad customer, and don't ever let down your guard against his taking over. In fact, your worse self is full of the old Adam. Several thousand years of so-called civilizing process has only coated him with a pseudo-niceness; and let's face it, under that thin coating he is amoral, unmoral, immoral, predatory, aggressive and every other adjective you can think of to describe human nature with gloves off.

And don't think you haven't got human nature in the raw in you, no matter how nice you are. It can get loose and mess up everything for you. The only safety element against this worse self is to get your best self into firm control and keep it there, for that best self does not derive from the old Adam, but from God. It is, in fact, the God in you.

So in liking yourself it is first important to like God, since God is within you by nature. As you come to know God you will know yourself better and like yourself more. And when I say that loving God leads ultimately to a normal liking of yourself I am dealing not in theory, but fact.

Read the following letter from Philip _____ who lives in the Bronx, New York City. Philip is a teenager and a pretty smart one, judging from his letter. Teenagers, as you may know, sometimes have a pretty awful time with themselves. Maybe it's growing pains and all that, but they sometimes go from elation to the depths of despair in no time at all. And when they get off the beam morally they really get fouled up. I have had more teenagers tell me, and mean it, that they didn't like themselves than almost any other group of human beings. But please read Philip's letter:

Dear Dr. Peale:

I have just read your latest book *The Amazing Results of Positive Thinking* and found it the answer to most of my problems, especially the chapter, "You Can Become Strongest In Your Weakest Place."

As a normal adolescent I have, and had, many doubts about myself. I felt inadequate, abnormal, useless, etc. Because of these feelings I went into the worst depression I have ever had. It was an unbearable torture. I felt rejected by everyone, even by God, because of my faults. I was so miserable that I even damned God.

But soon, I began to take stock of myself, looked at myself and emphasized my good points. I turned my thoughts away from myself and towards other people. I joined organizations and started to help others, and it was wonderful! I began to concentrate on my studies to strengthen my good points. I found that others began to like me more for all the things I did; I no longer felt rejected, and what's more, I liked myself a lot better.

I found God, and found Him in a new revelation. It was as if I had seen Him personally. I found a place in His world.

All these things came to me before I read your book. When I did read it, it gave me proof that I was right and that there are others who suffer also.

Let this be just another letter to be with all the rest confirming your philosophy on positive thinking.

No wonder Tolstoy said, "To know God is to live." One thing is sure, to know God is to love Him and this leads to knowing yourself and finally to loving yourself. This is only natural when you think about it, for if God created us He put Himself in us, as we have already pointed out. When you keep close to God you are in basic harmony, therefore, with yourself. But when you remain separate from God you are, in effect, getting away from your own basic self. Then you are in a strange and unnatural state of pseudo-self. This being an unnatural state you are just not content in it. And so after a while you actually get to disliking yourself, but what you dislike really is this phony self.

When, therefore, you return to God you are returning to your real self. You are back home at last in joyful association with the natural self you can like. That is just exactly what happened to Philip _____ from the Bronx. Now he likes himself and life is exciting and very happy.

Another factor in knowing yourself and therefore liking yourself is to esteem yourself. Self-esteem is vital to being successful as a person. Tennyson says, "Self-reverence, self-knowledge, self-control—these three alone lead life to sovereign power."

Self-esteem is one thing the personality simply cannot do without. It has long roots into the ego itself and, in fact, is actually related to fundamental identity. And to have one's basic identity depreciated, especially by yourself, is perhaps the greatest of all blows to the personality. Deep within human nature is a basic sense of sacredness regarding one's person. Most people do not think of this in quite such dramatic terms for there is a warped tendency these days to think of sacredness as "corny." But even so, there is a point of basic human dignity in every person which must never be offended. This is that inner area of consciousness where God is in you. If this is violated it represents an extraordinary and serious damage to the individual. When this happens to a person he suffers the most painful form of self-dislike and as a result the personality deteriorates.

Let me tell you of a very human drama, one that illustrates how loss of self-esteem may bring on an acute self-dislike, so acute that it led almost to self-destruction. Happily the story also contains a positive cure. I believe it will mean more to you if I let this woman tell the story in her own words, just as she wrote it for our magazine *Guideposts*. It is anonymous, of course.

> It was autumn; the hills around the town where we lived flamed with scarlet and gold. But I was past caring about the season. All through the long, hot summer, a sense of guilt and unworthiness had been festering in

me. The reason had a stark simplicity. The previous spring I had done something wrong. I had been unfaithful to my husband.

My husband didn't know. No one knew, except the other man . . . and I was no longer seeing him. Perhaps there were extenuating circumstances. Perhaps not. The fact was that I had broken the Seventh Commandment, and from that moment I hated myself. I went to church. I prayed. I asked God to forgive me. But I could not forgive myself.

I said nothing to anyone; I was too ashamed. But I was not so sure that the man in the case was being equally silent. I began to imagine that a certain coolness had appeared in some of my friends. I thought I sensed an aloofness in our mother. I became sure my guilty secret was a secret no longer.

As the summer wore on, my morbid imaginings grew more acute. On my birthday, I remember, someone sent me a greeting card with best wishes for "a happy occasion." The word "a" happened to be capitalized, and printed in red ink. To me it was the scarlet letter: "A" for Adultress. I tore up the card with trembling fingers.

My upbringing had left me with a stern and demanding conscience—too stern, too demanding. Now my reason, my sense of values, everything was crumbling under its relentless pressure. I could not think—I could only feel. I lost weight. I could not sleep.

My husband urged me to see a doctor, but I refused. I was beginning to think that my husband also knew my secret, and was afraid that if I went to the doctor, he, too, would know, would do or say something to reveal his conviction that I was unworthy, unclean, unfit to be a wife or mother. I lived in hell, a hell of my own making.

It was something my husband said that triggered my final act. He was reading in the newspaper about some woman who had deserted her family, had run off with another man. "Good riddance," he said. "They'll be better off without her!"

I felt the icy fingers inside me tighten: my husband was telling me that he knew my secret—and that he wanted to be rid of me.

There can be a terrifying logic in a disordered mind. The woman who had run away with her lover, I reasoned, was more honest and less hypocritical than I. My husband thought she deserved to lose her family. What punishment, then, should be meted out to me, whose whole life had become a lie? I asked myself this with agonized intensity, and somewhere inside of me a voice seemed to answer like a muffled bell tolling: "You're no good to anyone. You're bringing disgrace on your family. You ought to remove yourself altogether. Then they could start a new life, without you."

Without a word to anyone, I went upstairs and packed a small suitcase. I took a length of string and lowered it to the ground from the bedroom window. I came back downstairs, walked past my husband, went into the kitchen, let myself out the back door. I went downtown and registered under an assumed name in the town's tallest hotel.

My room was on the fifth floor. I was afraid it wouldn't be high enough. I walked to the window and looked down. The street below was dark, but I could see the lights of the traffic. I was terrified of dying, but the voice inside was louder, now, fierce, inexorable, telling me that I was unfit to be a member of the human race.

I sat down at the desk and wrote a note to my husband, telling him that I loved him and the children, but that things would be better this way. I wept as I wrote it, but I wrote it. The voice kept telling me to hurry, hurry. I opened the window and closed my eyes; I didn't dare look down. "Oh, God!" I said out loud, and turned around, and sat down on the sill, and let myself fall backward into the empty darkness.

I fell five stories, I waited for the impact of the pavement, for nothingness, for oblivion. Instead I smashed into the top of a parked convertible. I went through the canvas roof, into the back seat. I felt an agonizing pain in my back and legs. Then I fainted.

I came to in a quiet hospital room. I tried to move, and couldn't. I was encased in plaster from the waist down. A man in a white coat was looking down at me. Quite a young man, with steady, sympathetic eyes. "I'm your doctor," he said. "How are you feeling?"

A wave of despair washed over me. I was still alive, such a miserable bungler that I had failed even to do away with myself. Even death wouldn't have me. I felt hot tears sting my eyes. "Oh, God," I said. "God forgive me!"

The young doctor put his hand on my forehead. "He will," he said calmly. "Don't worry about anything. We're going to help you learn to love yourself again."

Love yourself again. I never forgot those words; they were the key that opened the door of the prison of self-hate that I had built around myself. They contained the truth that ultimately made it possible for me to rebuild my life.*

This is an extreme case of a person who hated herself so much that she could no longer tolerate herself. Fortunately not many suffer so acutely. But there are vast numbers of people who are afflicted with a similar personality problem in less degree. They are not right within themselves and as a result they have lost much of the pleasure they once had in living with themselves.

But there is no need for anyone to continue in this unhappy

* *Guideposts*, April 1960: "Love of Self" by Marguerite C_____, pp. 14–17. Carmel, N.Y.

condition of mind. The way out is first, to want out and second, to get some help from a good counselor, a minister, a spiritually wise friend, maybe a doctor or a psychiatrist, the latter if he has some spiritual understanding. If he hasn't don't touch him with a ten-foot pole.

Third, do some real basic praying, of the kind that calls upon the saving grace of Jesus Christ your Saviour. Just tell the Lord honestly that you are fed up with yourself as you are and don't want to be as you are anymore. Tell Him you can't seem to do anything really constructive about yourself and so you are turning to Him to do with you just what He thinks you need. God will always answer an honest, humble and trusting prayer of that quality. He will set in motion in you that creative three-point process: self-releasing, self-finding, self-esteeming. Then you will start liking yourself again.

So whatever you do keep your self-esteem right up to the mark.

The third element in the formula which the young pastor was given in that back room "consultation" described at the beginning of this chapter is this: Learn to let God run your life.

I realize that a person reading this, who has little or no background in our kind of thinking, might wonder a bit; indeed, might even write this off as some queer kind of religious stuff. Well, let me say that it is not queer; it's simply a down-to-earth way of saying that if you haven't done so well with yourself or your life, let someone into the driver's seat who knows how to do it. Move over, as it were, and let the Lord take the wheel. He will keep you on the road and get you where you want to go; namely, to a happy, successful and useful state of life.

Naturally, a person isn't going to like himself very well

when he is in continuing inner conflict, when frustration takes the joy out of life, or a sense of guilt haunts him. When your mind is cluttered up with gripes, resentments, hates, grudges; how can you expect the mind to produce joy, peace and contentment?

Anyone who thinks at all cannot help knowing that you can get out of the mind only what has first been put into it. If you are not happy, or not doing well, or if, to put it bluntly, you are messing things up for yourself, the chances are you are under poor direction. Your mind isn't delivering control, power or know-how.

The technique is just as simple as this. First, make yourself humble. That may be difficult, especially if you are not used to being humble. Most of us have quite a lot of false pride in us that keeps us insisting, boastfully, that we can run our own lives and need no help from anybody. But run them where? Often right into the ground, so to speak, or in a more accurate description into trouble, failure and personal unhappiness. It is very important to get humble. I'm sure you can be that big, for only a big person can be humble. The little fellows don't even know what humility means. It is not a virtue of the small fry. It is reserved for the big in *mind*. But you are in that category. How do I know that? Because you have read this far in this book. If you were not reaching for something big you wouldn't have lasted to this particular page. You would have passed it up for a T.V. western long before this.

Step number two is, having become humble, talk straight to God. No pious business—talk to Him as your friend who is going to pull you out of yourself and get you going down the main highway to success and happiness.

A friend of mine, a robust two-fisted fellow, "wobbled" to use his own description, through forty-one years of accumulating dislike for himself. Finally as he put it, "I came clean with myself, telling myself the harsh honest-to-Pete facts about myself. Then one night I went out behind the garage and leaned on a fence looking up at the stars. Something began pulling at me and suddenly, believe it or not, I found myself praying out loud. I didn't even close my eyes and I certainly didn't kneel. I just looked God straight in the eye and said, 'So what, God, I'm licked. I can't do a thing with myself; You take over and do whatever You want to do with me.'

"That was it," he added, "and I've never prayed since that time with my eyes shut. I don't want to look half asleep when I'm talking to God."

Well, that is perhaps a curious quirk but maybe it's not too bad a method of praying, for I recall reading in the Bible: "And the Lord spake unto Moses face to face, as a man speaketh unto his friend." (Ex. 33:11) Rather man-sized religion!

At any rate it worked. A new direction began to show and this man started going places, all kinds of places: personally, family, business. He likes himself much better, but he has not lost that humility, that humble willingness to let a Big Hand take over at the controls. This then is the cure of self-dislike.

What unhappiness we do bring upon ourselves by stubbornly continuing in our inner conflicts and outer ones, too, when it just isn't necessary to live in such conflicted manner. The secret is simply: let God take over and run your life. This will make it possible for you to live and like it because, with God firmly in charge of you, you will have so much less trouble with yourself. And therefore you will like yourself so much better. You will become a tough-minded optimist about yourself.

Sum-up of *Like Yourself—at Least Most of the Time*

1. Learn really to know and esteem yourself.

2. Cultivate a self you can trust and believe in.

3. Picture yourself as the kind of person you wish to be, affirm that you are that, then practice being it.

4. Keep some inspirational dissatisfaction as a goad to self-motivation. Complete self-liking dulls the drive factor.

5. *Your* self is well named. It's yours for keeps. You're stuck with yourself.

6. Since you have to live with yourself it's important to develop a self that's pleasant to live with.

7. Love God and you will develop a normal respect and regard for yourself.

8. Learn to let God run your life. You'll like the results better than your own self-management.

9. Be humble, be big in mind and soul, be kindly; you will like yourself that way and so will other people.

FIVE

HAVE PROSPERITY
AND ENJOY LIFE

I'll have to admit it, and actually I'm not averse to doing so, that much of the prosperity I've had and a great big share of the joy of life are because I married right.

Marry wrong and be you man or woman you are in for a lot of headaches. Marry right and your life will be full of joy; and prosperity too.

They say that many a man would have been an outstanding success had he not had a nagging, complaining, unsacrificing wife who wouldn't play on his team. The reverse is also true that many a woman would have contributed greatly to a family's prosperity and joy had she not been forced to carry along a mixed-up, ineffective and disorganized husband.

When two people, husband and wife, combine their lives loyally, each to the other, and build that relationship solidly upon spiritual principles, they create one of the greatest assurances of prosperity and enjoyable life known to man.

My wife and I decided at the outset to be a "team" each putting in his or her best to the joint enterprise of cooperative living, each supplementing the other's weaker points by compensatory strength. We decided also to build our joined life-team upon the Lord knowing, as the Bible so well says, that "except the Lord build the house, they labor in vain who build it."

Of course, most of the shoring up of the Peale family has come from my wife, Ruth. She has always been a tough-minded optimist. She was only twenty-three years old when we were married but she had a spiritually mature idea which she put forward from the very beginning, namely, that if, confidently, we would put our lives in God's hands and sincerely serve Him, and if we would love and help people, not forgetting to work hard, He would always take care of us.

Believe me, this was no theoretical idea with her. She believed in it as naturally as she breathed the air. And we lived on this belief, too, because not only was it a basic creed of her life but, in a practical sense, what else could we do? Personally, in those days, I had my doubts about such ideas. It was my opinion that God helped only those who helped themselves; in fact, I believed that the best way to be sure that God would take care of you was to take pretty good care of yourself.

You see, I had been to Boston University School of Theology where they didn't go in for any such simple kind of faith. They pooh-poohed stories of naive souls who put a trusting faith in the Lord to help them in practical affairs and were sustained thereby. The so-called miraculous element in religion they just couldn't see at all; the main thing was an ethically patterned Christianity designed to facilitate the rise of left-wing panaceas which was what they smugly called "intellectually respectable" religion.

They were good men, who taught and studied there, and many of them had come out of the homes of old-fashioned plain people, and while they had a tender nostalgia for the uncomplicated faith of their fathers, they had proceeded so far into religious and sociological sophistication that the idea of God helping anybody in a way that smacked of the supernatural to any extent was considered reactionary. And, of course, I went for this assuredly "intellectual" point of view, hook, line and sinker. Ruth had her problem with me on this score.

Her faith was completely unalloyed. It was the real thing. Faith, you may recall, is the substance of things not seen. That applied perfectly to our situation. Ruth had hardly two nickels to rub together when we were married. She had stayed out of college for awhile, working for the Michigan Bell Telephone Company to get her older brother through school. Then he went to work to help her meet her own college expenses. After graduation, she took a teaching position in Syracuse Central High School in order to help her younger brother to graduate.

I had a fair salary as pastor of a church in Syracuse, but was paying off the heavy debts of my own education and was putting my younger brother through college at the same time. I had worked my way through Seminary running a dumb waiter in the Boston Y.W.C.A. I was referred to by fellow students as the "dumbest waiter" the Y.W.C.A. ever had. I'll buy that, but at least it was better than putting out money for meals, especially when I, too, had only two nickels to rub together.

I had saved no money, that's for sure, and we began our married life on the proverbial shoestring, a well worn one at that. I recall one night during the great depression in the early thirties when funds dropped so low that I went out and walked up and down in the park with a feeling of actual desperation clutching at me. But Ruth was never even phased. "The Lord will provide," she said, "let us just keep on serving Him and trusting. He will give us fresh insights and ideas which we will turn into workable plans."

Well, thirty years have passed since then and never yet

have we missed a meal. (Probably wouldn't hurt if we did.) We have had nice homes with all of the necessities and some of the extra comforts. We have raised and educated three children, not one of whom ever gave us any trouble, only joy. We have traveled in many parts of the world. We have been given some extraordinary opportunities for service and have been blessed by the friendship of many and by the love of not a few. Ruth was right; indeed the Lord has taken care of us. We have had a generous share of prosperity and enjoyed life, though we have also had our hard knocks. I've long since come around to Ruth's faith in God's providential care. I had to, for I witnessed it working not only in our own experience, but in the lives of hundreds of others as well.

Ruth probably did not know it at first, but she had stumbled onto one of the greatest laws in this world of law. It is called the law of supply. In fact, neither she nor I had ever heard that term until many years later, when it was used by Dr. Frank Boyden, Headmaster of Deerfield Academy, one of our outstanding schools for boys. Dr. Boyden had built this great institution from practically nothing. Today its plant is one of the best in the educational field.

"How did you do it?" I asked admiringly as he told of the adversities and close brushes with bankruptcy over the years.

He chuckled, "I'm sure the bank wrote me off a hundred times; but funds always came. Time and again we were scraping bottom but it always came."

"How?" I insisted.

He turned a face full of faith toward me and said, "Through the law of supply. I was doing something God wanted done; making men out of boys. I was doing my best; I sought and followed God's will. I put everything in His hands and I worked my head off. All of this stimulated the law of supply and it's still flowing."

As we drove away from Deerfield after this conversation,

Ruth kept repeating, half to herself, "the law of supply—the law of supply, why that is just what I have been practicing all my life. I never heard it named but that is it—the law of supply. This is our big secret of living, Norman," she said sort of awestruck.

"It's yours, honey," I said softly. "I hope some day to go for it myself one hundred per cent as you do."

I had to struggle to believe and accept this faith in a law of supply, and even as I write these lines I must confess to incompleteness in practicing it. Fortunately I have Ruth to practice it for me. But as to the reality and workability of the law of supply, I now have not the slightest doubt—nary a doubt at all.

How does this law of supply work to produce prosperity and stimulate well-being, creativity and enjoyable living?

First, it is the conviction, the absolute unshakable conviction, that the supply will always be sufficient, not necessarily abundant, but always sufficient.

Admittedly this conviction is not easy to come by, especially if you have been taking a dark view of things for a long time. And dealing with that dark view habit is precisely the first place to start. You must become a tough-minded optimist. Muster up your character, you have some you know, and start practicing the bright view. It will pay off, I assure you. When I visit London, I always go down Fleet Street and up a narrow way to a quaint old restaurant, the Old Cheshire Cheese. Well known to thousands of American travelers, it is famed for beef and kidney pie, delicious roasts of beef and mutton and incomparable English cheese.

One corner of the restaurant is famed as the spot where Dr. Samuel Johnson dined each noontime, meanwhile pouring out wit and wisdom to a delighted coterie of friends. One day he got to discussing the constrictive effect of depressive attitudes. Banging his fist on the table he declared, "Egad, it's worth at least one thousand pounds a year to have a bright point of view." By that calculation in our money, it is worth nearly three thousand dollars cash to banish a dark and desolate cast of mind.

So, take the bright view that if you do your part, the very best you know how, and always think and work positively, the supply will come.

Always remember that gloom chases prosperity away. Prosperity shies off dark and inhospitable minds, veering away from the type of mind that is filled with shadows and doubts, for doubts tend to reproduce themselves in doubtful results.

Practice until it becomes a part of you the conviction that the law of supply is actually at work in you. Of course, simply having the conviction will not guarantee results; but let's put it this way, without the conviction as a base the other important factors in the working of this law will not operate.

When finally you have this vital conviction deeply rooted and firmly established in consciousness you will no longer waste precious energy in worry and agitation. You can go about your daily job in the secure knowledge that all things are working together for good, your own good and the good of everyone who comes into contact with you. You will now become really creative. From the new creativity operating in you, fine things will happen. You will no longer take flops, or at least so many of them. It's *most* exciting. Furthermore, the law of supply operates equally well whether you are working with little or with more, or even much.

Ruth tells of the frugality she had to practice in her college days. Yet she belonged to Alpha Phi Sorority, the oldest and we modestly thought the best sorority on campus. Always being a natural-born business woman, she was elected house manager and so got her board and room. And she was in lots of extra-curricular activities, too. She had a wonderful time on practically nothing.

One day an examination of her pocketbook revealed just thirty-seven cents, and where any more was coming from was not clear, but was she worried? Not at all, for did she not live on the law of supply, the law of prosperity? That evening she wrote her weekly letter home and it bubbled with happiness, as her letters always do. Just incidentally she happened to mention that she was "really rich for I have thirty-seven big round cents. But that doesn't bother me. I've been lower than that."

Her brother, then selling out on the road, "happened" to be home at this time and read her letter. "Strange," he remarked, "I have been thinking lately that I would send Ruth a little something. Guess now is the time. So it was that a few days later the shrinking thirty-seven cents was augmented by seventy-five dollars from brother Chuck. Ruth took it as a matter of course. "My, my," she said, "what in the world will I ever do with seventy-five dollars?" But I know what she did with it; she spent some of it on necessities and saved the rest. She is a terrific combination of religious faith and free enterprise.

Only recently Ruth pointed out that the law of prosperity-supply is still working, even though the demands as well as income are a bit higher than in the old thirty-seven cent days. It seems that Ruth had to write some checks totaling several hundred dollars. You see, she keeps the family books, does the banking, pays the bills, even handles the income tax. (She taught mathematics in high school and has a natural business head.)

So this day she had bills totaling a rather large figure, but she didn't have that much in the checking account. She might have dipped into savings, but if you do that, they aren't really savings. Besides, she would have felt it necessary to take that move up with me, and she wanted to avoid disturbing what is optimistically called my "literary" activity, meaning this book. Confidently she wrote the checks that evening but did not put them in the mail. She knew something had to be done by the next morning and wasn't at all surprised, though she was pleased, to receive in the morning mail a check for money owed us that was just a few dollars short of what was needed. It was the old thirty-seven cents—seventy-five dollars equation all over again. The sum was different, and considerably more, but the principle involved was the same regardless of the amount involved.

One of my friends who thoroughly believes in this principle and who has inspired me over the years is Eugene Outerbridge, a bulb grower in Bermuda. There is a definite dynamic spiritual quality about Eugene which derives, I'm sure, from his complete dedication to God and his humility as a disciple of Christ.

Every year for many years he has "preached the gospel" at Eastertime in our church in New York City by flying up over seven thousand Bermuda lilyheads timed to burst forth in all their glory on Easter morning.

Eugene is a great believer in the law of supply which is indeed a definite working principle in his personal and business life. He has the faith to believe in miracles. Let him tell of his experience with this tremendous spiritual and practical law.

"Came the loss of my business and I had to start anew. One day there was a sight draft to meet: only $287.60, but no money was available. Being a firm believer that God helps those who help themselves, I got out my ledger, looked up some likely accounts and went out to collect; but not one cent could be collected. At dinner I was tired, and perhaps a little blue, when my wife said, "Why don't we turn it over to God?" Then and there we did just that.

"At 8:30 that evening there was a telephone call from a large hotel; someone wanted to see me on business. Within half an hour I was there and was met by the attractive wife of a man in a wheel chair. I was thanked for coming at such an hour, but understanding that I was a florist, the man said he wanted to send certain flowers to different friends, and would I take care of the various orders? 'Add it up, please, so that I can give you my cheque.'

"That night I drove home in renewed faith, a never to be forgotten faith that God answers prayer, because I had in my possession a cheque for $286.00, only $1.60 short of the amount of the sight draft due in the morning.

"Another time $4,000.00 was needed in my business. Letters were written, telegrams were sent to accounts that owed me money, without results. Two weeks later, still praying and working, a cheque of 900 pounds (practically the amount needed then) came from England, an account I had written off, but God knew of it."

I realize this philosophy of life may be doubted and even attacked, and if the reader desires to dispute it by saying, "It ain't so," that is, as they say, "O.K. by me." But I have seen this sort of thing happen so many times in the experiences of my wife and in the lives of others that I have long since decided not only to take stock in it but to try and live on it myself. I do not understand many of the laws of nature, but I live by them just the same. Understanding may not be as complicated as it appears. This world was created and is sustained by a generous God, who must want the best for all His children since He put so many best things into the world.

He made it so that the bountiful supply will come to us to cover our necessities if we keep ourselves in harmony with God and His processes. This is no get rich device for it won't work that way. The desire for riches and more riches tends to shut off the line of communication with spiritual good. It is conceivable that the practice of the prosperity-supply principle might add a considerable accumulation of money. But in this case it would be at the cost of fundamental blessing itself and the final net accounting would be against you.

The law of prosperity-supply was never intended to produce a superfluity of material values unless with it is given a spiritual direction as to its use. And one's accountability for it must remain clearly in harmony with what we know to be God's will. You may grab all the money you can get your hands on and live with no spiritual concern whatsoever, taking care of yourself to full extent and you may get away with it for quite a while, but of this solemn fact you may be dead sure—God always pays off. Sometimes He does not pay quickly but He pays, which is to say that if you despiritualize the law of prosperity-supply you had better look out for something in your life, something that means a lot to you, to go sour. It is only natural if you put a sour quality in, you are just bound to get something sour out ultimately.

There is nothing at all wrong with having money unless money has you. But if God has you, really has you, then you will be interested in circulating and using money for Godly ends. Then along with the money will come an amazing surplus of all kinds of blessings direct to you and through you to the material and spiritual economy to keep the wheels of creativity going round. Putting it in a nutshell, it is my belief that money used with little or no concern for God or humanity is sour money and will go bad. But money used with spiritual responsibility is good money and will continue to flow abundantly in the prosperity-supply pattern.

I have actually helped a good many people to have more money if I say so myself. And I have done this in many cases by teaching them to give. It would be impossible to tell you how many people have told me enthusiastically, "I started giving fearfully, thinking I didn't have very much and that it was dangerous to give on the level you suggested. But do you know something? The more I gave the more I had." One stenographer put it this way, "As I give more my purse fills up more. It's beyond me and I was never happier in my life." How right she is. This girl became so happy that she became radiant and beautiful and one day along came the man she had dreamed of. When I married them he said to me, "Something about her got me. She is terrific." That is true, but I recall that she was actually rather dull and prosaic until she embarked on the give-yourself and give-your-money program. Strange thing, the more you give it out, the more it comes back, but not always in dollars and cents.

Sometimes it flows back in rich values with just enough money to meet needs. My mother-in-law, for example, came of good Christian people in Canada, just the kind of honest folk you find in church, not a fancy country clubbish church of suburbia, but a plain small town type of church. She married a young preacher and he had only small churches all his life. Late in life he preached Sundays and worked in the Ford plant in Detroit weekdays. Today the little church which they say "he saved from going under" is one of the big churches of the area. He was always a gracious, courtly man with the peace of God on his face because it was in his heart.

Grandpa and Grandma Stafford always had to scrimp and make do and try to make ends meet. The law of supply brought them only a small quantity of money, though enough; but I have seldom known people who had such an abundance of blessings. Their three children did so well. "Chuck" has a responsible position with the Chamber of Commerce of the U.S. Bill heads personnel in a big New Jersey concern and is treasurer of *Guideposts* magazine, and I believe I am not immodest in terming Ruth a top church lay leader of our time.

Grandma and Grandpa Stafford had the love of hundreds of people into whose lives they entered lovingly and creatively. They never lacked any necessity though he drove an old Ford car for years and a new piece of furniture—well I really don't

59857

recall any. I asked Grandma, now 85, if she believed in the law of supply. That was a new one on her but as I explained it her face brightened, "Oh, you mean God's generous goodness. I've lived in a perpetual shower of blessings. Of course, I believe in that law of supply. What a nice name for it."

Then there is my old friend Ralph Rockwell. One day nearly twenty years ago Ruth and I bought a little farm in Duchess County, New York. Ralph Rockwell came of good Connecticut people who had worked hard all their lives, the kind out of whom the USA was made. He had been a butcher, drove a milk truck and now he wanted to supervise our farm. "I'm your kind of folk," he said, and I knew at once that he was.

From that day on he "used the place as if it were his own." To me he was always "Mr. Rockwell." "I'll run the farm, you do the preaching," he said, and while I don't know too much about preaching, I know even less about farming, so followed the advice.

Then the years added up and the work was too much, so Mr. Rockwell retired and his son Elliott took his place and he, too, is my friend. When I want a piece of delicious chocolate cake I drop into Mrs. Ralph Rockwell's house. This lovable, motherly woman usually sends us out from her little house with a kiss as well as the cake.

They have lived all their lives on God's supply line. And blessings surround them in their older years as they have all along the way.

So you see we must not make the mistake of concluding that prosperity is necessarily or even usually to be conceived in monetary terms. An old hymn gives perhaps the best of all descriptions of true prosperity. "There shall be showers of blessing sent by the Father above." This is the secret of having prosperity and enjoying life, the unshakable conviction that God will take care of those who love and trust Him. And He will too.

Nor does this imply or even infer freedom from struggle and difficulty, even hardship. One thing is sure, you can't have the sweet in life unless also you have the bitter. And the solving of problems is sweeter by reason of the struggle. But the essence of the matter is that the believer in the prosperity-supply philosophy successfully comes through all difficulty. He may, to be sure, come through plenty but the end result is the important thing—he comes through; and, we may add, he gets a lot of fun out of life while coming through. It can indeed be said the way of the tough-minded optimist may often be hard, but it's good too—mighty good.

To add to the first, namely, the conviction that the supply will always be sufficient, is an equally important second step in stimulating prosperity, and that is never to think lack or talk lack. Emerson told us that words are alive and if you cut one it will bleed. A word is simply a thought eternalized. Georgiana Tree West states it very well indeed, "When we think about a thing we are forming a pattern of that particular thing; when we speak about it we are sending forth the word and it is being condensed into form. We should not speak of an idea unless we want to see it take form in our life. In the Old Testament," she continues, "is the promise, 'Thou shalt decree a thing and it shall be established unto thee.' Our word is a decree. When we say 'I am poor,' we are decreeing poverty. The more emphatic we become the more evidences of poverty we shall see in our life. Our word is the expression of our mental image. God's laws establish it, bring it into manifestation."

In other words it is the part of wisdom not to think or talk lack for the danger is thereby to actualize lack.

Charles Fillmore warns "do not say that money is scarce; the very statement will scare money away from you. (Note that the only difference between the word scare and scarce is one letter *c*.) Do not say that times are hard with you; the very words will tighten your purse strings until omnipotence itself cannot slip a dime into it. Do not allow one empty thought to exist in your mind but fill every nook and corner of it with the word plenty, plenty, plenty."

These may seem rather strange ideas to the person who has not considered the amazing power of thoughts to create or to destroy. The reason Emerson used the curious figure of a word "bleeding" is because he recognized that the thought behind words can give life or death to our hopes and our desires. Lack thoughts and lack words tend to produce lack in fact, while prosperity thoughts and words move us in the direction of prosperity.

We have recently celebrated the sixteenth anniversary of the founding of our magazine *Guideposts*, the most widely circulated non-profit inspirational interfaith publication in American history. Edited by a board consisting of Jews, Catholics and Protestants, it has soared above one million circulation and is read monthly by several million persons.

Guideposts has never carried advertising, depending upon volume circulation to meet its costs. Its purpose is to publish true life stories of people who have overcome fear, failure and defeat through the power of God in human experience and the opportunity inherent in American freedom.

Back in 1945, *Guideposts* was only an idea in the minds of a few people. The need for a publication of this sort was obvious, but to inaugurate such a magazine required capital, experienced people and a staff of topflight writers. We had no capital, no experience, no writers. All we had was an idea, some convictions, some faith and a lot of stubbornness. So we began the "magazine" as a small four-page folder. But the stories it contained had meaning and appeal. The total amount of funds with which we began was the astronomical sum of seven hundred dollars.

Gradually the subscription list grew to twenty thousand.

We were using as a publishing plant a dwelling house owned by Lowell Thomas located on Quaker Hill, Pawling, New York. One night the house was destroyed by fire within the space of an hour and the entire subscription list, of which stupidly we had made no duplicate, was lost. So there we were in a most unpropitious position—no plant, no offices, no subscribers. But Lowell Thomas told the story on his radio program asking our subscribers to notify us. Our friend DeWitt Wallace of the *Reader's Digest* carried an article along the same line. Result: we soon had not twenty but forty thousand subscribers. That's one fire that paid off.

Publication continued in unbroken sequence, but mounting costs imperiled the already shaky condition of *Guideposts*. Bills accumulated. Our supplier threatened to cut off paper delivery. We were increasingly in a bad way, and not only were we thinking very gloomy thoughts concerning the project, but our gloom was expressed in such statements as "We can't last long this way; we are sure to fold," and other similar destructive evaluations. We were at that time anything but tough-minded optimists.

We reached out desperately for every possible source of support. A trickle of gifts kept the presses rolling. But continuance was a touch and go basis, very precarious. Then I called a meeting of the discouraged and frustrated staff. You may have sat in upon negatively conditioned meetings, but I cannot imagine a more gloomy gathering than this one. The entire conversation was a dismal and dull emphasis upon the difficulties facing the publication. Whatever would we do with that stack of unpaid bills on the table? This magazine at that moment was all but defunct. Only a miracle could save it.

And that is exactly what happened. *Guideposts* was saved by a miracle. It was a miracle of fresh, creative thought surging up through re-stimulated and re-energized minds. I mark this particular moment of time as one of the great experiences of my life. I learned something that day that literally changed the course of my life.

To this staff meeting we had invited a woman who, on a recent almost as desperate occasion, had contributed to *Guideposts* $2500 cash money. We hoped that lightning might strike twice in the same place. She listened quietly to our dismal recitation of the discouraging plight of our publication. Finally she spoke up, "I get the notion," she said, "that you gentlemen expect me to make you another contribution. Well, I might as well put you out of your misery. I'm not going to give another nickel, in fact, to underscore it, I'm not going to give you even one more cent."

This did not put out of our misery, but, on the contrary, more deeply into it. She was, you might say, our last straw. Now, even that was gone. We sat enveloped in gloom.

Then that gloom was pierced by the bright light of creative thought that changed everything because it changed us. This woman said, "I will not give you money for it would be of little value in the failure pattern in which you are sunk. But I will give you something of far greater value than money." This astonished us for at the moment we could think of nothing that had greater value than cold cash.

Then it came, the miracle that saved this enterprise from failure and which has revolutionized a good many people since then. She said, "I will give you a fresh, dynamic and creative idea. With it you can solve your problems and get all the material resources you need," and she made good on this promise, too, believe me. Prosperity flowed.

"Now," she continued, "let's take a straight look at your situation. You lack everything, do you not? You lack money, you lack equipment, you lack a sufficient number of subscribers, you lack ideas, you lack faith. You are in a lack situation. Do you know why you lack all these things?"

Then she answered her own question. "You have been persistently thinking lack and you have thereby created a condition of lack." This struck me at first as a strange line of approach, but upon reflection its reasonableness became apparent. We did lack, there was no doubt about that. We lacked
everything. And it was also true that our thinking and talking
had been in terms of all that we didn't have, upon what we
could not do. So, grudgingly, we admitted that she was right,
but even so, it was hard to accept the thought that thinking
lack could result in lack. But there were those unpaid bills
right there on the table. You couldn't laugh them off.

"All right, now," she went on, "enough of that. We are
going to stop thinking and talking lack this very minute. I
want you to flush those lack thoughts out of your minds."

"But how can you do that?" I asked. "You cannot open a
hole in your head and flush thoughts out and you cannot tell
thoughts to disappear just like that."

She glared at me. "You can do anything with your mind
that you really want to do. Plato said, 'Take charge of your
lives, you can do with them what you will.' So take charge of
your minds and in the name of the Lord command the evil
spirits of wrong thinking to leave you. Start now flushing out
those lack thoughts."

A dead silence fell and we sat for at least ten minutes
"flushing out lack thoughts." Incidentally, that is a good plan
to follow every day. Take a few minutes daily to flush out the
old, tired, dead thoughts. Empty your mind of them. Don't
let them bog down and harden in your consciousness.

"Now," she said brightly, "your minds are empty," and she
added mischievously, "that's not unnatural either. All that
mass of lack thoughts is cleaned out. But we must quickly fill
your minds or they will sneak back in again. We must fill your
minds at once with prosperity thoughts."

She turned to me, "Norman, how many subscribers do you

need to keep *Guideposts* going successfully?" I thought quickly and said, "One hundred thousand would do it."

"All right then, let us fix the figure of one hundred thousand subscribers in our thoughts. But first let's ask if we have prayed about this project, have we dedicated it to God and to human service? Are our motives unselfish and genuine?"

We searched our souls and answered those questions in the affirmative. We must realize that nothing that is wrong can ever go right. Right results are never inherent in wrong attitudes and wrong purposes. You have to be right to get things to go right.

Then our friend went on with her dramatic treatment of our uncreative mental condition. "I want you to visualize those hundred thousand subscribers to *Guideposts*. I mean see, *really* see them. Look out there until they are clearly pictured, not by your eye, but by your mind." We must have looked foolish trying to picture ourselves as having one hundred thousand subscribers when the books showed only forty thousand. But it wasn't nearly so foolish as to sit around moping and talking ourselves into failure as we had been doing.

Suddenly like a flash we did see, clearly saw deep in consciousness a vast number of people whom we were to serve and help. It was most astonishing. We saw *Guideposts* going ahead to a tremendous future of service to those people. I quite forgot myself (which incidentally was exactly what I needed to do—forget that old defeated self) and cried out excitedly, "I see them. I see them."

She looked at me approvingly, "I really believe that you do. That's great. Now that we see them, we have them. Let's pray and thank God for giving us one hundred thousand subscribers."

I was hardly prepared for this, but I'm willing always to pray with anyone at any time, and I joined the lady in prayer.

Privately I thought we were pushing the Lord pretty far.

In that prayer she thanked God for giving us the hundred thousand subscribers, for the new turn toward success and for the prosperity He was showering upon us. She ended by quoting "Whatsoever things ye ask and pray for believe that ye receive them and ye shall have them."

The prayer finished, I looked around expecting everything to be changed; but there was the same old stack of bills still on the table. I half expected them to be gone, miraculously paid; but there they still were. Everything was the same, that is, except the people around that table. They weren't the same. They were strangely different. It showed on their faces, in their demeanor, but principally in the vital new thoughts that began to eat away at those hard problems. New power was operating in us. We could feel it. We were changed and so everything began changing for the better.

That was back in 1945. Today *Guideposts* has over one million subscribers and nearly twelve hundred firms take it for their employees. You will find it in hundreds of hotel rooms placed there for the inspiration of guests. Two hundred people find employment in its business and editorial offices. Its message has deeply penetrated American life, lifting people up, always up, persuading them and showing them how to live upon God's great power. It has developed thousands of God-powered people in our country and abroad. It has fused men who believe in God into a common spiritual enterprise dedicated to a free America and to brotherhood. Indeed it is one of the most effective inspirational interfaith publishing enterprises of all time. The experience of *Guideposts* has taught that a simple secret of effective living is to empty out lack thoughts and refill with prosperity thoughts and to keep on the beam with God all the way.

Never think lack—always think prosperity. Always build your life and thoughts around God. Love and serve Him and add to that the love and service of human beings and you will know the best in life. The tough-minded optimist joy-fully lives on God's great law of supply.

Sum-up of *Have Prosperity and Enjoy Life*

1. Learn to live on God's law of supply.

2. Cultivate a bright point of view. Dr. Johnson said it's worth $3,000 a year to any man.

3. Do your honest best, think right and the Lord will, for a fact, provide. He will do the providing through you.

4. God will always take care of those who love Him and trust Him and sincerely do His will.

5. Prosperity is not always or even usually to be conceived in terms of money, but as a constant flow of God's blessings.

6. Never think or talk lack for in so doing you are decreeing lack. And lack thoughts create a condition of lack.

7. Stress the thought of plenty. Thoughts of plenty help create plenty.

8. Thoughts and words form your mental image. And since we become what we picture be sure your thoughts and words express prosperity and blessing rather than poverty and defeat.

9. Every day flush lack thoughts out of your mind and re-fill with dynamic thoughts of abundance.

SIX

KEEP THE MAGIC OF
ENTHUSIASM WORKING
FOR YOU

While out of town on a speaking trip I dropped in on a Rotary Club luncheon to "make up my attendance," as is the rule among Rotarians. Selecting a table at random I introduced myself to the other men sitting there and was a bit taken aback when one of them growled, though in rather jocular manner, "So you're Norman Peale, eh? Well, I hope you can do something for me. Sit down and start spouting wisdom."

It was evident that he wasn't quite as rugged as he sounded —just one of those diamond-in-the-rough types, you might say. I found him to be a very likeable man who had a sort of bantering or challenging way about him. "Now don't hand me any of that positive thinking stuff," he continued, "because I'm sunk, washed out, dragging bottom and what have you." So ran this ultra-racy but completely out-and-out confession. He didn't seem to care at all who listened in for he boomed this out in a foghorn sort of voice that all and sundry couldn't help hearing.

"I'm completely out of enthusiasm and enthusiasm is what you are always trying to sell. And don't think I haven't read all your books. I've got 'em all. I like them too and they're on the ball, but just why they haven't clicked with me I don't know. So where do we go from here? How can I pick up this enthusiasm and get going again?"

I let him have it straight right from the start. He wanted an answer and since he wasn't backward about speaking right out, neither was I nor did I care who heard me either. So I said, "What you need—is God."

This really rocked him and you could have cut the silence around that table with a knife. However, a couple of fellows across the table had a look on their faces which showed I wasn't playing a lone hand. I expected a ribald comeback which seemingly would have been in character; but then you never know what really is in character, that is to say, of what the real man is made.

When finally he spoke it was to say quietly, "Maybe you've got something there. But just make the connection for me between enthusiasm and God, won't you?"

"Sure will," I said and taking a menu from the table I printed on its blank side the word *Enthusiasm* in large letters. "Ever study the origin and derivation of words?" I asked. "You'll learn something if you do—something you never knew before. Where do you suppose we got that word enthusiasm that we all bandy about without delving deeply into its meaning?"

"How should I know," my fellow Rotarian grunted. "I've never studied words, but I can see a point when one is made, so what's your point?"

"Well," I replied, "the word enthusiasm comes from two Greek words EN and THEOS. The first means IN and the second is the Greek word for God so actually the word enthusiasm means IN GOD or in another rendering, FULL

OF GOD. So to go back to your question as to how you can get and hold enthusiasm, the answer is get full of God and stay that way."

"Going to preach me a sermonette?" growled our friend, but actually there wasn't as much growl by this time.

"Why not? You asked for it. I didn't bring it up—you did." At this the two fellows across the table chimed in with affirmatives and we had a rousing session there at the luncheon table on how to make enthusiasm work for you. Beneath that assumed tough exterior this man really wanted something.

Enthusiasm can work for you and its absence can equally work against you. This is a fact because of the immense importance of spirit in successful life performance. Whatever happens, whatever losses you suffer, if you don't let your spirit sag or collapse, your comeback capacity will keep working; and all of us have this comeback potential. But when your spirit cools, then your personality may become brittle and, whereas before you could withstand even the heaviest knocks, now comparatively insignificant blows can crack and even break you.

In a brass foundry I watched molten metal at 2200 degrees being poured out of huge crucibles made of some translucent material which when hot glowed like fire. The foundry superintendent who was showing me about took a huge sledge and holding it in both hands delivered powerful blows against a hot empty crucible. The best he could do was to put almost imperceptible dents into its sides. Then he picked up a small hammer and approached a crucible that had completely cooled off. With a short motion only from the wrist he tapped the cold crucible and shattered it.

"Nothing can break these crucibles when they are hot," he said, "and anything can break them when cold." Then he added, thereby revealing himself as a philosopher of sorts, "It's pretty hard to break a man whose spirit is hot; but even small things will bust him wide open when his spirit goes cold."

That was a good way of saying that lack of enthusiasm works against you whereas it's like magic when working for you.

Now I am not going to promise you that enthusiasm, the kind which really goes to work for you, is some superficial quality you can pick up and exploit without putting yourself to too much trouble to get it. The fact is that getting it may involve a rather comprehensive process of re-education. It may, and perhaps will, mean a thorough overhauling of your thought pattern. It will certainly require practice because it is an acquired skill to a considerable degree. Fundamentally, as previously indicated, enthusiasm in depth is actually spiritual in tone and content. This is precisely the reason I advised our zestless friend at the Rotary Club luncheon that he needed God. If you want an enthusiasm that will work for you I must tell you in all honesty that you will also need God.

Perhaps we had better expedite that emphasis by giving you a clear rundown on exactly what we mean by needing and having God. I think the best way to communicate this concept to you is in the form of one man's experience; and the man I'm thinking of is my friend Fred R_____.

Fred was the rather disorganized son of a substantial father who had a fairly good small business. He always did have charm of personality and a real good mind; but beneath his carefree attitudes he was not very happy. It so happened that a friend called up and asked him to go to New Haven one night to a big meeting at which the missionary E. Stanley Jones was to speak. "Me go to hear a missionary! Don't make me laugh," said Fred. But his friend insisted and Fred liked to please his friends.

But Jones got to Fred, really reached into him, and when he asked all who wanted to go deeper into the spiritual life to remain for a private meeting, Fred was the first to accept. Before the meeting ended he had committed his life to God. Seems awfully fast, I agree, and the skeptic might well laugh it off as superficial and opine that it wouldn't last—at least not with Fred; a fellow like that wouldn't stick.

A fellow like what? It doesn't follow at all that a man is what he seems.

Dr. Jones told his new converts that a first step in the new life was to go right out and go to work spiritually. Fred was always on the ball and he showed up at the Methodist minister's home early in the morning.

"Who's down there?" asked the sleepy pastor from an upstairs window.

"It's Fred R—— and I've got religion. I want to start working. Come down and open up!"

"Why don't you get religion at a respectable hour?" asked the minister quite guiltless of any humor.

"How about some coffee?" asked Fred. And cracking some eggs into a frying pan the two men were soon seated across the kitchen table, the pastor still in a mild state of shock. He just couldn't believe what he saw, that strange light on Fred's face. He had, of course, always believed in conversion. Could it be that this careless young fellow had actually met Jesus Christ?

Out of that kitchen conference things began happening to a church, and to a town, and to innumerable people.

The pastor hardly knew what to do with the unleashed enthusiasm of this zealot, who kept clamoring to the pastor, "Let's get on the ball and stop fooling around with Christianity." So the pastor appointed Fred as a member of the official board. At the first meeting he heard the treasurer dully report that the church had a current expense deficit of some $8,000. He leaped to his feet.

"This is a disgrace," he shouted. But the older members

remembered Fred when—and they bristled. But he overrode them. "Let's start underwriting it right now."

"They had to pony up," explained Fred afterward, "because I shamed them by taking quite a chunk myself." He raised that deficit in just a few days of laying it on the line among the members. He ruffled a few feathers but there was something about this flaming soul that rather made people wistful. It had been a long time since they had been up against a really transformed human being. Some had never seen one in all their churchgoing experience.

Fred organized a businessmen's spiritual discussion group which met one day weekly for lunch. He effectively transmitted his own experience. The town began to feel the impact.

Then he went after teenagers. He formed a class that met on Sunday mornings where again Fred hit every problem of young people and I mean every problem head on. The kids loved it. For twenty-five years he has turned out some of the finest men and women you ever did see.

One night on a plane flying to California I met an attractive young business man. He hold me of his job, leadership in his community and all that his church meant to him. "Where did you get this enthusiasm?" I asked.

"You ought to know," he said. "I got it from Fred R_____. I'm proud to be one of his boys," he said with misty eyes—or maybe it was that mine were misty.

Once a year he brings his class in a busload to my church in New York to hear my sermon. I got used to it later, but I'll never forget the first time he brought his young people. He hardly knew me but he phoned and said, "Hi there, Norman, my batteries need recharging and so do my kids, too. I'm bringing them down Sunday so, for heaven's sake, have something on the ball." He denies that he ever said it this way, but I have a good memory.

Fred R_____ is by all odds one of the greatest laymen I've

ever known and one of the finest human beings as well. He has enthusiasm that really enthuses and he got it straight from God. So that is what I mean when I equate enthusiasm with God. Fred demonstrated the dynamic formula; enthusiasm equals EN THEOS (full of God).

My bringing God into the enthusiasm formula does not stem from any mysterious, complicated reason. It is simply that God is the life force from which, or from whom all life comes. As the Bible puts it: "In Him was life . . ." (John 1:4) and again: "For in Him we live, and move, and have our being . . ." (Acts 17:28). God is life so if you do not have God in you then your life force is at low ebb. And when you have life you will then have continuous enthusiasm of the type that has real potency, vitality and power—in short, the kind that gives meaning and happiness to the entire project of living.

How can anyone feel less than enthusiastic in this exciting, action-packed world? What a pity there are human beings whose lives are uninteresting to them. Unlimited reserves of ever new zest for living are available to all. And I am constantly meeting people who have discovered this wonderful fact.

One spring day I traveled a couple of hundred miles by car with one of the most enthusiastic, vibrantly alive men I have encountered anywhere. The weather that day was curiously changeable, bringing warmth, cool breezes, varying clouds, showers and golden sunshine in rapid alternation. The countryside was clothed in spring freshness. The road we were following undulated up hill and down dale.

At every turn my companion found some cause for delight. "What is more beautiful . . . ," he asked, indicating the fields we passed. "What is more beautiful than a flock of sheep in a green meadow like that?"

A few minutes later, marveling at long shafts of sunlight

piercing down through heavy overcast, he exclaimed, "Looks like a light from heaven, doesn't it?"

And the next moment, with a wave of his hand in the direction of a handsome old brick house set amid stately pines: "Ah! There you have early America at its best!"

Noticing a little stream splashing down a hillside and under a little bridge, he remarked about the beauty of "clear, cold water surging over clean washed rocks."

Great dark clouds came billowing up from the horizon, and he drew a deep greath of rapture saying, "Just take a look at the rugged grandeur of that sky!"

At length we stopped for gasoline. I found myself wondering whether my exuberant friend would find anything to trigger his admiration in the rather ordinary-looking service station. Sure enough—along one wall of the building three lilac bushes stood covered with lovely blossoms. Now, for me no flower has greater charm than the lilac. Each year I look forward to its springtime blooming. But never have I heard anyone as ecstatic about a lilac bush as this amazingly zestful man.

"I have seldom met a man with as much enthusiasm as you have. How do you have so much?" I asked.

"Guess I'm having my own springtime—sort of a spiritual springtime. I have been reborn." He explained that he had had a new religious awareness and experienced God as a reality. He quoted St. Paul's great words: "We also should walk in newness of life." (Romans 6:4)

"That's what I'm doing," he grinned.

"You sure are," I agreed.

I have watched so very many people come alive through enthusiasm that I must confess I'm enthusiastic about enthusiasm.

Enthusiasm releases the drive to carry you over obstacles which you could otherwise never hurdle. It tones up your physical vitality and keeps you going even when the going is hard. It invests the ups and downs of daily life with comeback strength and adds significance to all that you do.

Enthusiasm is wonderful. It gives warmth and good feeling to all your personal relationships. Your enthusiasm becomes infectious, stimulating and attractive to others. They love you for it. They go for you, and with you, too.

People often object to this line of thought and say: But what good is there in knowing all this if you just don't happen to feel enthusiastic? You can't have enthusiasm by simply saying you have it; you don't become enthusiastic by deciding to be, just like that!

But that is just where they are wrong, very wrong. You can *make* yourself an enthusiastic person by affirming that you are just that, by thinking enthusiasm, talking enthusiasm, acting out enthusiasm. You will become enthusiastic, really so. When you associate with enthusiasm long enough it grabs you and takes over within you.

This is based on a simple psychological law. There is a deep tendency in human nature for us to become precisely what we habitually imagine ourselves as being. It is the act of image-ing or picture-ing. Hold certain images in consciousness and like a sensitive photographic film the exposure takes. We can actually become what we picture. In fact you can be dead sure that at this very moment you are what you have imaged or pictured over many years. If you are lacking in enthusiasm and happiness just take a mental re-run and add up all the dull, despondent, negative pictures of yourself which for so long a time you have fed to your sensitive consciousness which is always ready to do your bidding. Only that can come out of a person which that individual has first put into himself. When will we finally catch on to the tremendous fact that we make or break ourselves by what we do to ourselves by the images we hold?

So use this affirmation daily several times: "I think enthusiasm, picture enthusiasm, practice enthusiasm." Do this for one month, and don't weaken. If you do slip, start again at once. Keep at it and you will get the surprise of your life. And everyone around you will be astonished and pleased because you will be so very different when enthusiasm really goes to work for you.

Having prescribed this treatment to many people I have, of course, no doubt of its effectiveness. Take hold of enthusiasm, do it deliberately and it will take hold of you and everything you deal with as well.

Personally I owe a great deal to the application of these principles and techniques in my own experience. By nature I was a negative, scared person overawed by my own painful self-doubts. But fortunately for me I was reared in a home that was packed full of enthusiasm. We didn't have much of this world's goods. The biggest salary my father ever had when I was growing up was four thousand dollars a year, though they were bigger dollars in those days. But you would have thought we were the richest people in the world—we were because we had a mother and father who loved life. It fascinated and charmed them. They saw beauty and romance in everything.

For example, as I write these lines I am on a train riding through the fabulous Frazer River country in Colorado. It is a glorious February day. I look out at blue skies, a few floating clouds of fleecy white and the whole tumbling mass of Rocky Mountains covered with snow. From train side to the far flung magnificent panorama of noble peaks, diamonds seem to glisten on the deep, soft snow. The tall stately pines are snow festooned as though some giant hand had sprinkled them with tufts of cotton as we do our Christmas trees.

It brings to mind a much less spectacular valley in southern Ohio and a winter's afternoon long ago when my father was pastor of a little country church and I was accompanying him to a Sunday evening service. We rode in a buggy behind old "Duck" our faithful white horse. Snow was whipping across stubbled corn fields and drifts were piling high along the fences. The road was almost indistinguishable. "Gosh, Dad, it's going to be a terrible night," I said. "There won't be anybody at church and how in the heck will we get home?"

Then my Dad started to describe the "glory and might of the storm." He dwelt upon the power of the elements, the lonely loveliness of the white landscape. He pictured the snug warmth inside the little farm houses along the way with blue smoke rising from kitchen fires. He was a great preacher and I loved to hear him talk to a congregation. He was thrilling because he was himself always thrilled. But never did I hear him in better form than that winter twilight as he delivered a "sermon" on the majesty of nature in a snow storm to one little boy in a buggy on a country road.

When later after the service Duck floundered us home the storm had ceased and a full moon lighted up the whole countryside in silvery radiance, Dad gave me another talk on how storms always pass and "the glory of God shines through." Dad saw God in everything. Maybe that was the source of his amazing enthusiasm. As we drove up the lane to put Duck in the barn he said something I've never forgotten: "Always make yourself enthusiastic, Norman, and your whole life will be wonderful."

Well, I must admit I haven't always followed his advice but he planted a wise idea in me anyway, and in later years it developed. My business in life is preaching and speaking. I go through a lot of agony because I have always been nervous about speaking even to small groups to say nothing of large crowds. But the compensation to me is the thrill of enthusiasm when it bursts through the inferiority feeling when I get going on the platform or in the pulpit.

I'm not much of a speaker, that I realize full well, and what success I have had with it is not due to any great wisdom or training or scholarship. It's been due to a simple four point formula:

1. Sincerity, absolute sincerity. I believe one hundred per cent in everything I say.
2. Enthusiasm. I get thrilled with it—caught up in it —so I must, simply must convey it to the people. They just have to hear and I hope accept it.
3. I make it simple in language and thought form.
4. It must be interesting. How can the most thrilling material in the world be made dull!

Only last Sunday I was preaching on the topic "Enthusiasm Powers Successful Living." I told the people with all I had what a wonderful thing Jesus Christ could make of life for them. My time ran out and I had to stop. I always aim to stop in twenty-five minutes. Then the big congregation stood and sang that tremendous hymn "Onward Christian Soldiers" following which our organist, Charles R. Cronham, surged into that great hymn called the Doxology, "Praise God from Whom All Blessings Flow."

Well, I found myself so full of enthusiasm that I could hardly refrain from starting another sermon. I could not resist having another word so, while the congregation stood quietly awaiting the benediction, they were surprised to hear me say, "Friends, we have just sung two of the mightiest hymns of faith ever written. You are thrilled as I am. Right at this moment everyone is lifted in mind and spirit. The immense power of faith is alive within you. Go out now into the world and live on that power."

Believe me, enthusiasm was working for everyone in that church at that moment. In the effulgent light pouring in through the great stained glass windows onto the people I saw reflected on their faces another and inward light. It was an unforgettable moment. Churchgoing can be a thrilling experience. It was on that day.

I must say for my part that the power of enthusiasm has always worked for me, which is why I have urged other people to let it work for them also. If it could do what it has done for me with my meager abilities it can do much for you, too, that's certain.

It has been my privilege to talk before many conventions of business men and salesmen. I want to tell you about one salesman whom I met at a national sales convention.

He wasn't in the habit of going to conventions which, of course, are attended by men who want to perfect their performance, the real producers. This fellow did not have enough get-up-and-go to get to a working convention on his own power. Motivation was just what he didn't possess. He was there because he had a boss who cared about his men and who had actually staked this fellow to the trip "in the faint hope" as the employer put it, "that I could get this character activated. He has the stuff if only he had some zip along with it. Wish you would talk with him after your speech if you could take the time. Build a fire under him if you can."

"Better build that fire in him rather than under him, don't you think?" I replied.

While I was talking at the luncheon in the ballroom of the Conrad Hilton in Chicago, I saw my employer friend at a table down front. When he caught my eye he nodded cagily in the direction of the man next to him, as if to say "here he is—work on him."

This salesman, whose name was Frank, was obviously a likeable fellow—one of those genial relaxed men—but too relaxed and maybe too genial also. He listened to my talk and I felt that I got a moderate response from him. After the meeting he came up to the head table and on his own, though I suspected he might have been coached, wanted to know if we could have a little talk. I took him up to my room on the twentieth floor overlooking a magnificent panorama of Michigan Avenue and Lake Michigan. The sun was streaming in the windows.

"I'm a no-account salesman brought up here by my boss, a darned good guy, who is barking up the wrong tree in hoping he can make a producer out of me." So he opened the conversation.

"Negative thinker, eh?" I responded. "Self-depreciator with high accent on the will to fail." I talked rather to myself as though making an objective analysis (which I was doing).

"Say all that again please."

I repeated it adding "lethargic mental reaction, absence of motivating factors. Probably resents childhood and his wife doesn't understand him."

He started up in his chair. "I thought we'd never met. Who briefed you on me? You know me like a book."

"Nobody briefed me. Your boss spoke of you, but he believes in you, the Lord knows why. I don't see anything much to believe in, though." I hastened to add, "I know there is something in you that's never yet shown itself that might be worth believing in."

"Gee, you're a tough character. I thought ministers were gentle souls," he said.

"It depends upon the treatment required. We are gentle when gentleness is needed and tough when toughness is indicated. The object is to help the patient which in this case is you."

"O.K. I'll come clean with you. All that you say is true and then some but one thing I haven't been guilty of is any sexy stuff. I have been one hundred per cent true to my wife. I don't drink much. Actually I'm a pretty moral guy. I hate tough stuff and off-color language—I am a dull, apathetic, lazy lout and you are right about my parents and my wife, they are always trying to push me around." He slumped dejected in his chair.

"Well, here is your prescription," I said, scribbling it on a sheet of hotel stationery. I even wrote an ℞ as they do on medical prescriptions. "That means TAKE THOU," I said. "And remember, no prescription is worth two cents unless you take it as directed."

He stared at the paper: "Practice enthusiasm daily." He looked at me in bewilderment. "But I haven't any enthusiasm. I've got to get it before I can practice it."

"Oh, no," I said, "put the shoe on the other foot. Start practicing it and you will have it."

"But how do you begin? And say, I thought you would pray with me."

"Hold your horses. I'm not through with you yet. Prayer will get into this all right. How in the world do you expect to get your motivation stimulated unless you go to the main source of dynamism?"

So I started him on his first lesson. "Get up and walk around this room and start listing the things you see that bring out enthusiasm." He walked around and said finally, "I don't see a darned thing."

"You sure are full of blind spots. What are those two things you are walking around on?"

"Why, feet of course."

"O.K. Mark them down as number one. Just think of having two feet. How would you feel if you had only one or maybe none? There's nothing like two good old big feet especially when you have legs to go with them."

"Never thought of that," he said.

"Yes, I know there are a lot of things you have never thought of but you're going to change your mental processes. What else do you see?" I asked.

"My hands, arms, eyes, nose, mouth, head—I'm way ahead of you." Indeed he caught on fast. "Look at that sunshine pouring into this room," he exclaimed. He pulled the curtains aside. "And that great street out there and the blue lake beyond. I get the idea. It's just to start thinking enthusiastically about everything. That's it. Isn't it?"

"Yes, that's it," I said. "And as you practice doing this it will in time become second nature to you. Moreover, you will find an increase in acute sensitivity. You will perceive and feel with a fresh keen awareness. When this happens you'll know it all right; for then an exquisite happiness will fill your mind. This will mean you are alive at last and no longer fit your description of yourself as dull, apathetic and lazy. Enthusiasm will really start working for you."

"How about that prayer?" he asked as I prepared to take off for the airport.

"Sure, let's pray," I said. A silence fell between us. "Well, start praying," I prompted.

"Oh, you want me to pray? I'm not in the habit."

"No better time than now to get you into the habit," I replied. I knew he wanted to pray.

"Lord," he said hesitantly, "I don't want to be what I have been any more, and what's more, I'm not going to be. Thanks for everything. Please give me enthusiasm for my job, for life, for everything. Lord, You're wonderful. Amen."

"How come you added that last line?" I asked curiously.

"I don't know, it just came over me that He is wonderful."

"So are you, old boy," I said. "And as they say—you ain't seen nothing yet if you just keep on this enthusiasm program and I know that you will."

My object wasn't to make a good salesman out of an indifferent one. It was, rather, to help a half dead man come fully alive. I knew that as he learned to participate vitally in life he would be better able to communicate and so the selling would take care of itself. He had the necessary know-how; he was just lacking in the equally important how-do. But as he increased in enthusiasm people who had known this indolent, sleepy, half-awake man were astonished by the metamorphosis demonstrated in his new outlook and improved output.

Aeschylus, first of the great ancient Greek dramatists, declared: "Happiness comes from the health of the soul." Soul health involves good will instead of hate, outgoingness instead of selfishness, enthusiasm instead of cynicism, and faith instead of doubt.

Practice joyous daily enthusiasm. Practice appreciating God's world until you really do for a fact. Give thanks daily for your blessings. Get the habit of thinking happy thoughts. Go out of your way to make other people happy. There is your formula for real happiness and enthusiasm, and it will pay off, too.

So it's a fact that you and I are pretty much that which we practice. Practice negativism and you will get negative results. Why shouldn't you? You have made yourself an expert in negativism! Practice failure and you can quite surely count on failing. Practice enthusiasm in even the most commonplace things and presently the immense power of enthusiasm will begin working wonders for you.

In closing this chapter I feel duty bound to warn you that the changeover from desultoriness to enthusiasm doesn't necessarily come either easily or quickly. There is a word little used these days which you might very well centralize in your vocabulary. It is the word *persevere.* You can tell something about what is happening to a country by the change in emphasis on word usage. In the great days when hard-working, goal-seeking men were making the United States the tremendous land it became the important words were *honesty, work, save* and *persevere.*

These words have all had a pretty rough time of it in recent years and that could be one symptom of what's wrong with us. I'm for bringing them back into circulation. At any rate, it is a fact that in building enthusiasm and the quality of personality hospitable to it you may have to persevere. But the end result will be well worth the effort, however long and painstaking it may be. For example, the case of a woman who wrote me the following fascinating letter. This letter, written on feminine notepaper, featured red roses against a background of pale pink. Ordinarily I do not take to such fancy stationery. But when I had finished this letter I would readily have granted there was good cause for the festive touch of these roses. It was from a lady in Indiana who emerged from a long period of unhappiness and frustration into the joyful excitement of a transformed life. She wrote:

> "Eight years ago my life was in a negative state—and that is putting it mildly. Knowing that something must be done, I decided to dust off the Bible and have a regular hour for prayer and meditation. Soon after this I came across your book, *The Power of Positive Thinking*. I tried the techniques you outlined. For two solid years I studied, meditated, prayed, disciplined myself— and nothing apparently was happening."

Note that "two solid years." She was really demonstrating perserverance, wasn't she? How easily many people get discouraged with a program of daily effort before even two weeks are up! But this lady kept at it for two long years even though she still saw no results. That's really something, believe me.

> "Then one night, very late, everyone in bed," continues the letter, "when I was at a point where I felt I had done just about everything to improve situations . . ."

Here is the critical point, where the issue hangs in the balance, where the danger is greatest of losing hope and accepting defeat, maybe even losing faith in God and becoming bitter. When you are at your wit's end and the feeling comes over you that you've done all you can, what then?—Why that's just the time to persevere and keep on persevering. What did this lady do?

"I knelt down," she writes, "and cried out everything to God. I prayed as I had never prayed before. This wonderful peace crept over me and the warm glow of some kind of love enveloped me. As I later understood, I had reached a complete relinquishment, after a period of repentance and godly sorrow.

"I then saw many things clearly. The passages of Scripture with which I had saturated myself took on new meaning. The whole world seemed different. It was as if I saw trees for the first time, flowers and their fragrance; as though now I had an understanding of life itself.

"This experience changed my whole life. It was so wonderful that when I tell about it I sometimes forget to mention the physical healing that took place—so much more important to me was the healing of the soul. Three physical ailments were wiped out, two organic conditions and one functional one. The organic trouble had been so painful that I had been under barbiturates most of the time. But in the years since it has never returned.

"The next day I began a clean-up of my whole life, making retribution wherever I could.

"Now I actually feel joy even in the midst of perplexing situations, and I have a courage that amazes me. Fear is gone and I am sure there is a beyond, a very beautiful one. God enabled me to experience a rebirth or awakening of the soul that keeps growing and growing. My! how exciting life is!

"I try my best to be of help to other human beings, unhappy persons and see their lives begin to change."

Quite a letter, isn't it? This person found something that changed everything for her. When in this depth you bring yourself into harmony with God's goodness and discipline yourself and stay with it—really persevere, you will condition yourself so that God's power will flood your life.

Then the mighty power of enthusiasm will start working—really working for you. Result! Instead of being pushed around by life you will take charge of life. Things will be very different and very exciting.

Sum-up of *Keep the Magic of Enthusiasm Working for You*

1. Enthusiasm is a word meaning full of God. So to have enthusiasm fill your mind full of God.

2. Life's blows cannot break a person whose spirit is warmed at the fire of enthusiasm. Only when enthusiasm cools is he likely to crack up.

3. If you are out of enthusiasm get reborn spiritually. That experience will make you come alive. Study the Bible text ". . . we also should walk in newness of life." (Romans 6:4)

4. Every day remind yourself of your own ability, of your good mind and affirm that you can make something really good out of your life.

5. Empty out old dead thoughts and be reborn in mind and spirit. Rebirth refreshens personality.

6. Have an eye for the charm and romance of life and practice aliveness.

7. To have enthusiasm simply practice being enthusiastic.

8. You can make yourself enthusiastic by affirming enthusiasm and by thinking, talking, acting enthusiastic.

9. Start and end every day and in between times too, by thanking God for everything.

10. Persevere in your search for God. When you find Him zest and enthusiasm will fill your mind to overflowing.

SEVEN

FEEL HEALTHY WITHOUT
SLAVISH DEPENDENCE
UPON PILLS

Please do not get the idea from the chapter title that I am against pills and medicine. In fact I take some myself now and then. I am simply concerned about slavish dependence upon pills rather than reliance upon those basic resources of health and vitality which are to be found in right thinking and the healing power of faith. What we expect to do in this chapter is to show how some people have found health, vitality and increased strength through the application of right thinking, especially spiritual thinking.

One of these is a brilliant university student who had indeed developed a slavish dependence upon pills. A perfectionist, he had become the victim of a feverish tension—a malady which seems to be increasing among young people. But this boy found the secret of emotional and physical health as his letter indicates. He tells his own story so well that I quote his words:

> I am a college freshman enrolled in Chemical Engineering at the University of Illinois. All through my

high school days I was a perfectionist—working to maintain good grades and to save enough money to be able to continue my education. As a result of this I graduated first in a class of three hundred, received the highest science award given by my school, saved enough to go to college, bought a car, had plenty of clothes and spending money, and have been dating a wonderful girl, a member of the same church as I, who I am really crazy about. By all earthly standards I suppose I should consider myself as very fortunate, but I lacked the one thing I wanted most—inner peace.

When I came down here in September I started in immediately to duplicate my high school career. At the end of my first semester I had achieved a 4.8 average (on a 5.00 basis) but when I went home between terms my nerves were so bad that, at times, it was all I could do to refrain from trembling. My father insisted that I go to a doctor. I started taking nerve pills by the mouthfuls but still couldn't calm down. My personality actually all but collapsed.

It was at this point my mother gave me a series of your sermons, and then the miracle began. When I came back this semester I read your sermons as regularly as possible, and the inner peace and confidence I am receiving from them is truly unbelievable. My nerves became calm and I've never touched a pill since then. I have a package of pills on my dresser as a reminder of what used to be before I put myself in God's hands.

This young man is very generous in his references to my printed sermons (which, incidentally, are available to any reader of this book. They are issued three each month and mailed to some three hundred and fifty thousand persons in our fifty states and over one hundred foreign countries. If you would like to receive the sermons regularly simply write to Foundation for Christian Living, Pawling, New York and mention the notice in this book.).

The creative experience of this student, which I must say does not always occur with such seeming rapidity, nevertheless suggests the improvement in well-being which can be accomplished through a spiritual mental procedure which we call the practice of the presence of Jesus Christ in the mind. A definite revamping and reconditioning of the mind often results from a studied and deliberate use of this spiritual technique.

Let me tell you of another case. A businessman recently reminded me of our meeting on a train some years ago at a time when he was in an acute state of crisis and high nervous tension. He recalls how I had suggested this procedure of "living with Jesus Christ in his mind" as a corrective for his condition.

I recall the incident very well indeed. I was walking through the dining car to a rear coach when I noticed this man, whom I had known for a long time, at a table, drinking coffee and smoking. "Sit down," he said. "Have a cup of coffee?"

"Sure thing. How are you?"

"Not so hot," he said, "in fact I'm pretty shaky."

We chatted and I finished my cup of coffee and he suggested another. "No, one is enough for me," I said.

"Well," he growled, "I've got to have another." In my brief time with him he emptied two pots of coffee, or a total of four cups, and chain-smoked cigarettes. I noticed that his face was agitated, hands shaky and fingers fumbling; and I asked what the matter was.

"Matter!" he echoed. "Matter! It would be the matter with you, too, if you had a lot of people sniping at you and double-crossing you, and trying to undercut you and every other thing." He started telling me about his problems—complicated, mixed-up situations—or rather a mixed-up attitude toward problems. The chief gripe was that he was "entitled" to be president of his company but a man from outside had been brought in over him, he remaining as Executive Vice-President. This was really eating him at his inner control center, and the more he talked I was convinced that it was an important factor in his personality disorganization.

Then, "Waiter, another pot of coffee, please." Nervously he lit still another cigarette.

"You are not going to get your answer that way," I told him. "Good thing it isn't whiskey you're drinking."

"Where do I get my answer?" he demanded.

I knew that basically he was a religious man so I gave him a spiritual formula which had proved effective in other instances. I felt that an uncomplicated idea could counteract his destructive obsession. I advised him simply to start consciously and consistently thinking about Jesus Christ. "Where is this tense fretting getting you anyway," I argued, "except into an acute nervous state? To overcome it practice living with Jesus Christ mentally for as large a proportion of time as possible. Saturate your mind with His presence." I noted his surprised look.

"Really do this," I urged. "This suggestion isn't anything fanciful. Think about Him as many times every day as you possibly can. Fill your mind with thoughts of Him. Pray many times daily. As you walk or drive, or as you work, say brief prayers. Repeat His words, allowing them to settle deeply into your consciousness. As you make the Lord the chief subject of your thoughts the presence of Christ will actually and realistically take hold of you. This spiritual revamping of your thought processes will do much toward healing you of potential crack-up by inducing new control and peacefulness in your emotional reactions."

He thanked me politely, but I felt an absence of conviction, as I got off the train at North Philadelphia. He told me subsequently that he thought here, for sure, was another theoretical piece of advice from a theoretical preacher. What possible relation could Jesus Christ have to business problems, or how a person feels physically—never heard that in church.

However, his nervous state got progressively worse so he realized that he had to take action or else; so he decided to experiment with the method I had suggested on the train. This incident occurred some years ago. Recently this man said, "That technique of thinking changed my whole life. I was slow in accepting it and it was not easy to perform but I can honestly say that it made me much better mentally, physically and spiritually. It gave me mental control and that led to an improvement in my nerves and then physical improvement followed. I got hold of myself. It helped me to rethink myself." The validity of his spiritual experience was indicated by the wholehearted cooperation and friendly support which he gave to his company president.

And it taught him some realistic facts, too, as for example: "I saw that I wasn't ready to be President of my company and in fact even wondered at the directors continuing me in the second spot." Later when the President retired he was advanced to the position; but then he was ready.

"I found that the healing process described in the Bible is still valid," he told me, adding this insight: "I now realize that when I met you that day on the train my problems were not business problems. I was the problem. But it took me a long time to get wise to that fact."

The same healing power is ever available to all who want it enough to believe, to ask, and to build up the mind into a faith attitude that can meet the conditions for healing. Remember that Jesus Christ said: ". . . If thou canst believe, all things are possible to him that believeth." (Mark 9:23) The process of living with Christ mentally makes you able to believe with the extra faith required for extra results.

Present day disciples of Christ do not realize or appreciate the tremendous power He has given them. How pathetic that so many should actually crawl through life half awake, half sick, below par, all but defeated, tired, nervous, discouraged. That miserable sort of existence cannot be what God meant for you or for me. Listen to this amazing promise: "I give unto you . . . (power) over all the power of the enemy; and nothing shall by any means hurt you." (Luke 10:9) Why don't we take and live on that power?

Perhaps our failure is in part due to a lingering notion that healing through faith just does not happen in this modern era as it did in New Testament times, though evidence is constantly accumulating to prove that it does really. Still, some people who firmly believe that Jesus Christ healed the sick in the First Century find it difficult to believe that this same power operates today and especially for them. The age of miracles is past, they say sadly. Healing is now done through scientific medical means . . . (and usually they add piously) though faith helps. To them faith only assists the doctor; its chief function being to get the patient into a better frame of mind and thus in a mild way stimulate the healing process.

But Divine healing itself is "scientific" in that it is conditioned by law, spiritual law, the highest form of law. And healings do happen today. Consider the following letter from a woman whose statements have been verified as authentic:

> At a luncheon some six weeks ago at the United Nations Building Mrs. Peale invited me to send you the story of my husband's healing.
>
> Ray was born with very poor eye sight. He did not have any muscular control of his left eye. This eye had almost no vision and the right eye had poor vision. He wore very heavy lenses for reading and another pair for general use without which he was not safe, even around the house. Besides this, he had spells in his eyes which started in 'teen age, becoming more frequent through

the years, and very painful. Just prior to his healing they were coming on twice daily. For an entire year we had been praying that God would heal him.

It was the last Sunday of June 1954 and we had been listening to an Oral Roberts radio broadcast. At the conclusion of his prayer I said, "A man who has just been healed takes off his glasses." Immediatcly he pulled those glasses off. He has not needed glasses since then. He could see better without his glasses than ever before. The spells ended abruptly. The healing process continued for about five days. There was a feeling of expectancy each of those days as the various steps of the healing unfolded. First, the blurr left; then, after an hour and a half of twitching in his left eye, he found that he had muscular control of that eye; straight lines which had always appeared zig-zag now could be seen as they were; distance vision continued to improve.

What gave me utterance when I told my husband to take off his glasses because he had been healed? At that time I was puzzled and did not understand it. Now I know that it was the prompting of the Holy Spirit.

If this testimony can serve some useful purpose and help others to believe God, you may use it in any way you see fit. We have so many blessed promises: "What things soever ye desire, when ye pray, believe that ye receive them, and ye shall have them." (Mark 11:24) "Confess your faults one to another, and pray for one another, that ye may be healed. The effectual fervent prayer of a righteous man availeth much." (Jas. 5:16) "If our heart condemn us not, then have we confidence toward God. And whatsoever we ask, we receive of Him . . ." (1 John 3:21–22)

I am sure the Lord is more anxious to heal than we are to be healed. He would like to cleanse us from the inside out. Healing for the body and the soul were included in the redemptive act of our Lord Jesus Christ. What a wonderful Saviour we have!

Now of course you can cite cases of people who prayed for healing and did not receive it. So can I. In fact I personally have prayed for healing and did not receive it. But that does not mean that some others have not been granted this great blessing. If I pray and do not receive, it means simply that I am not praying correctly, or that there are barriers within me which block off the power or, of course, it could mean that I am receiving a "No" answer. If the latter, then I must obediently change my prayer to one for adjustment in which case I shall be given power to live with my problem and use it creatively.

Perhaps some who have received healing have been granted this great experience that their spiritual perception may be deepened and their souls grow larger in dimension. Take the case of my old friend H.S., for example.

Three years ago in Switzerland I received a letter from the sister of a man who had been a classmate of mine in high school. She wrote that H.S., her brother, had been medically examined and the verdict was incurable disease, with a prognosis of not many months to live. She asked me to pray for her brother to be healed which, of course, I did very sincerely. Weeks passed, and then months, and I heard no more.

More than two years later a speaking engagement took me to Indiana. Outside the convention hall a man walked up to me and said, "Hello, Norman."

I assumed he was an old friend but could not place him. "Where did I see you last?" I asked.

"You last saw me," he replied, "when we graduated from high school." Yes, it was H.S. He had read in the newspaper that I would be speaking that day and had driven from his home eighty miles away, just to say hello. "I have time for only a brief visit," he said. "I must get back. I'm really busy."

"Let me look at you, H.S. Two years ago in Switzerland . . ." But he interrupted to say that he knew about his sister's letter. Then he told me what had happened.

Shortly after the verdict of incurable disease he had returned to the clinic for further tests and had to be helped out of his car. The doctors made no secret of their belief that he might not be able to get home again. Then he decided not to fight it longer but to surrender everything to God: his fear, his life, everything. "God had been good to me," he said. "And however He wanted it was all right with me. I just told God I loved Him," he concluded simply but with great feeling.

Then one afternoon alone in his room he suddenly felt very much at peace, as if completely surrounded by the love of God. He had a strange feeling that God had given him a new lease on life. Before dinner time he made up his mind that he was going to leave the clinic and return home the next morning. The doctors were very dubious, but at his insistence discharged him. He drove alone all the way home, seven hundred miles. The exertion did not affect him. "I have felt fine ever since," he asserted. "And two years have passed."

Instantly a question rose in my mind whether this perhaps was only a temporary reprieve. Apparently H.S. read my thoughts for he said, "Yes, maybe it's only temporary. But isn't all life temporary? It doesn't matter so much to me now how long I live. I have had the glorious experience of God's healing presence and I now know that I am safe in life or death. That is what matters to me now."

Surely there is no greater good fortune in human life than this state of mind to which my old friend had come—it is a depth of security that nothing can disturb despite whatever comes. Actually there is only one real security in this world, only one; identification of the soul with the ultimate reality— God, our refuge and strength. This is the only sure security. And H.S. had found it.

Faith works in another way to give health without slavish

dependence upon pills. Faith stimulates a powerful determination, a massive *will* to be healthy. This can give a quality of well-being greater than might seem possible under some circumstances.

Many have an inadequate concept of the healing, strengthening force that may be summoned from within ourselves by powerfully motivated will. Indeed any emphasis on the power of the will seems rare today. In the old days we heard much about will power. Young people were taught to develop it and no one was considered strong at all who did not evidence will power. It was considered a sign of manhood. But will power in most of us has become flabby like a muscle long unused. The disciplines of faith can, however, put tone and resiliency into your will once again, and with it working efficiently you have a valuable ally in creating good health.

One night I went up to Kingston, New York to give a talk and was met at the Poughkeepsie railroad station by an old friend Bob C. I had known Bob C. since my Syracuse days back in the twenties. He had served in the State Police where he had a fine career which ended when, chasing a criminal, he overturned a motorcycle at high speed and was banged up very badly.

He recovered, however, but had some stiffness. He took over the operation of a motion picture theatre. All went well until one morning he could hardly get out of bed. He became for a while so crippled that assistance was required to get him up in the morning and stand him on his feet. Once started he was able to keep going by sheer power of will but not without great pain.

One day his doctor said, "Bob, let's face it. I am terribly afraid that you are going to become totally incapacitated. I'm as sorry as I can be but you are entitled to the facts and I can't lie to you."

"O.K. Doc," said Bob. "You just go on doing all that you

can do with your medicine. I know you will do everything possible and you are very helpful, but I am going to turn this case over to another doctor, the greatest one there is, and get this straight, Doc, I am not going to be an invalid, not me."

He told me this story as we were returning to Poughkeepsie after my lecture. I can see him yet standing under the station platform lights, the snow slanting through the mellow glow. I could hardly conceive that this strong man had ever passed through such an experience as described. "Walk up and down for me, Bob," I asked. With scarcely a suggestion of joint or muscular impediment he strode up and down before me. "How do you explain this wonderful thing?" I asked, amazed.

"I had a good doctor, one of the best; and I had the greatest doctor of all and with His help I just used something else, something He built into me."

"Meaning what?" I asked.

"Meaning will power," he replied. "I just willed not to be an invalid. I would not even consider it. The Lord helped me to endure the pain and to keep the old joints and muscles going."

"Have any pain now?" I asked.

"Sure, a little but that's part of the deal and I can take that. It doesn't stop me either. When the joints pain me a lot I just tell them to forget it and keep moving like they're supposed to do."

The train for New York covered with heavy up-state snow swept into the station and I waved to Bob as it pulled out. He was standing straight and tall; quite a man I thought, a terrific mixture of faith and will power. One thing is sure he had no slavish dependence upon pills. He took them, of course, but he put greater dependence upon the power that had been "built into him, will power." And he, of course, had plenty of faith power to go with it.

Many people rely heavily on pills rather than upon vital

thoughts to improve their health. But it is a known fact that thoughts can do much to make you either sick or well, or half sick or half well. Right thoughts stimulate health; wrong thoughts encourage and in some instances actually cause illness. One physician told me: "Some people are actually draining back into their bodies the diseased thoughts of their minds." Asked to specify these diseased thoughts, he replied, "Oh, the usual. Fear is certainly one; and so is guilt. Another is gloominess or despondency. Of course one of the worst is resentment. That really makes them sick. In fact if fear and resentment were eliminated from people's minds I believe our hospital population would be reduced by maybe fifty per cent. Certainly by a lot anyway."

The ill effects of resentment become understandable when you consider the basic meaning of the word resentment. It is derived from a Latin word meaning to feel again. For example, suppose someone does you an injury. Your feelings are hurt. You go home and say to your wife, "Do you know what he did?" And as you tell her, you re-feel your hurt. In the night you may awaken and again remember what he did— and so you re-feel it once again. So it goes: everytime you resent you re-feel the hurt.

By the time you have repeated this a few times the grievance has lodged itself in your unconscious as a "sore" spot that does not heal. How can it heal—when by resenting or re-feeling you keep it inflamed? There it remains as a sore thought subtly affecting your general feeling tone. Perhaps this is why we say, "What he said made me sore."

In time the effects of sore thinking may extend to your body, too. As a result you may develop any one of the numerous physical ailments which doctors now recognize as psychosomatic—that is to say, originating in the mind or feelings. Such is the high cost of ill will or that sore thinking called resentment or re-feeling. The cure comes by discontinuing the re-hurting thought.

The best course is to arrest resentment quickly before it really gets started. When someone hurts you, immediately put spiritual "iodine" on the mental and emotional wound. Apply to the hurt the generous attitude of understanding and forgiveness. Talk to yourself something like this: "I'm sure he didn't mean it." Or, "He isn't himself." Or, "I'll skip it." In this way, while you may be hurt, you are hurt only once. You will avoid prodding the wound to make it sore and inflamed until finally it becomes chronic.

And when anyone hurts, irritates or angers you, it helps to begin praying for the offending person immediately. This isn't easy, of course, indeed it may require strong self-discipline, but such prayer effectively pulls the sting and soothes the wound in your mind.

Ill will is well named for it literally means the unwell personality. Healthy-minded people have a well will because they have learned not to re-hurt themselves by resentment or re-feeling.

I once gave a talk at a meeting in the baseball park in a Pennsylvania city. Months later I was told of a woman who said she was saved from a nervous breakdown that night in the ball park meeting. Her exact words were: "As Dr. Peale put his hands on his head and said, 'Drive all unhealthy thoughts out of your mind,' something powerful happened to my thinking. I was suddenly freed from my unhealthy thoughts."

This reference was to a gesture I sometimes use in picturing the healing hand of God as resting upon the head and casting out negative and debilitating thoughts. It seems indeed strange that in an instant the cumulative thought-build-up of years could be broken down and emptied out, but the result proved that such a miraculous change had occurred. But perhaps we call such a happening miraculous only because we do not as yet understand the laws effecting such change in mental and physical states.

Since God created the mind He is certainly able to correct a mental condition in one dramatic act if He so wills. The fact that such healing does not often occur in this sudden manner does not at all mean that it cannot happen. In this instance and in others about which I have substantial evidence intensified spiritual power instantly revised long-held unhealthy mental patterns and produced conditions of well-being.

Usually the process of revamping a thought pattern to attain better health is much less rapid but on the basis of results no less dramatic than that of the woman at my ball park lecture. Thought change requires in most cases a good many ups and downs of encouraging progress and discouraging retrogression; but if the desire and effort are maintained a permanent improvement from unhealthy to healthy thinking may be anticipated. Indeed, the change in the way you feel can be quite remarkable, as was the case of a man whom I met at a dinner.

I attended this dinner with a dozen men members of a committee. One of these men was by all odds one of the best story tellers I ever listened to. He had the rest of us roaring with laughter. He was a gay and effervescent personality. I pulled out some of my own supposedly sure-fire stories and they got a fair to middling response but nothing like the way-down deep laughter his jokes brought forth. Studying this remarkable raconteur I noted that he threw himself with everything he had into every narrative. One of his stories I had myself told years ago and wouldn't have thought of using it as it was too old and shopworn; but he got a terrific laugh with it. It was the way he put himself into it that put it over so charmingly.

As I listened fascinated to this attractive personality I noticed a minister at the far end of the table grinning at me and shaking his head as if to say, "What a guy!" Afterward this minister asked, "Well, what do you think of our jovial friend?"

"Quite a man," I replied. "A very remarkable man. He seems alive way down deep."

"Sure," he declared, "he's one of our best exhibits."

"What do you mean exhibits?" I queried.

The pastor then went on to explain, "You should have seen this fellow a few years back. Never a smile out of him then. He carried the weight of the world on his shoulders. He was a sour-puss if there ever was one and people actually hated to see him come around and start spouting his pessimism.

"He made money, plenty of it. In fact he put together a big enterprise and employed several hundred people. He always was a real good businessman. But he got no pleasure out of it for he was becoming a crabbed, mean, irritable old man years before his time—if there ever is such a supposed time."

I couldn't imagine that the man who had just been the life of the party could have been the negative, unhappy individual the pastor described.

"He got to feeling sick too and little wonder with all those sick attitudes of his," continued the pastor. "He began to feel some pain in his chest and arms and was a bit breathless at times. The doctor warned him to ease up: that his blood pressure was not quite normal. He developed a sick psychology and haunted doctors' offices. Other aches and pains developed. The usual psychosomatic symptoms appeared."

The pastor chuckled and continued his interesting account: "One doctor shipped him off to a specialist in Chicago and there he really got it. This specialist went all over him, gave him all the tests, then said: 'Your pains are not real but pseudo and they come not from faulty heart action but from wrong thought action. In other words, there is nothing very wrong with you physically that couldn't be O.K. if you only got your thinking straightened out. In some way the life has been knocked out of you and you had better get it built up or else.'

" 'Well, how do you do that?' our friend asked.

"The doctor looked him over for a long minute and said, 'Better go home, go to church and get some honest-to-God religion!' Yes, sir, believe it or not that's exactly what he said. Then he added: 'That's my prescription; fifteen hundred dollars, please.'

" 'Fifteen hundred bucks for what?' he shouted.

" 'For knowing what to tell you,' the doctor quietly answered. 'You charge plenty for your services, don't you?'

"Well that man came home and immediately came to see me," the pastor continued. "And was he mad; called that specialist a hold-up man and everything. He told me he would get fifteen-hundred dollars' worth out of it if it killed him. And, What in the devil did that doctor mean by sending him to a minister to get religion! Of course, I explained the powerful effect of wrong thinking on the physical body and gave him some counseling and spiritual treatment—the kind you outline in your books. It was a fairly long process but he kept coming and followed directions. You see, he had paid through the nose for advice and what motivated him most at first was simply to get his money's worth. But he soon got beyond hating the specialist, whom he now thinks is a great man. The doctor sized him up correctly: knew if he charged him a big fee he would think the advice important and treat it seriously. At any rate he found God and God found him and you see what he is now."

So, it is a fact that you can feel healthy, without slavish dependence upon pills by getting your thinking into the way of being cured by God. A doctor in Vienna calls this process "logo-therapy" meaning healing by God and says that in

Europe many are sick simply because they have lost the meaning of life. And this, of course, is no less true in America. Pills have their place, even a very important place; but there are some ills that pills cannot reach (to use a play on words); some that only God can heal. Actually God is performing the healing even when pills are used for He made the material out of which their healing property is drawn. Healing by naturalistic scientific means is not really divorced from the spiritual.

The importance of healing the mind and the attitudes is repeatedly illustrated in the experiences of modern people. Amos Parrish, the prominent merchandising expert, was riding in a New York City taxi cab when the driver happened to mention my book, *The Power of Positive Thinking.*

"How do you know about that book?" Parrish asked.

"Because it saved my life," the driver said.

"How did it save your life?"

"Because it saved the mind of my wife—and that certainly saved my life, because without her I'd be through. My wife was very confused. The psychiatrist at Bellevue told me they couldn't do anything more for her. But they recommended I get her *The Power of Positive Thinking.*

"I went down to Macy's that afternoon and got it. I read part of it to her and finally it seemed to be getting through to her. So I read more. In a few weeks she could read it a little by herself. That was three years ago. She now has read that book many, many times—maybe 20 or 30 times. She knows part of it by heart.

"Well, she got the big ideas it has—and that saved her mind. Therefore it saved my life, and I believe hers, too."

Mr. Parrish says, "I told the driver I was going to see you. With tears in his voice, the driver said, 'Oh, how wonderful! Please tell him how thankful we are to him for saving our lives.' "

Of course, much as I appreciate the driver's high regard it was not I who "saved" his wife's life. I personally never saved the life of anyone. However, I am humbly grateful that I could be used as an instrument to help this woman. That God's healing power got to her in such an effective manner is evidence that the spiritual can transform the mental and vitally affect the physical state. There is a form of thought which, when it penetrates and lodges in consciousness, is the most powerful mental and spiritual force operating in this world. And that is positive thought about God; that God is not only your Creator but your re-creator as well. He made you in the first place. And when you have misused or misdirected that which He made, namely yourself, or life has done things to you, the great fact is that He can make you over again.

Mr. Parrish with whom I shared the platform at a meeting of salesmen in Memphis, Tennessee wrote me later to tell of an experience which happened while in that city. He said:

"Down in Memphis you had a *Guideposts* meeting at noon. A whole army of men were there. Many came up and spoke to you. We heard one of them say, 'Thank you for saving my life!' You spoke to him for a moment, then as he turned away we went after him.

"We heard you tell Dr. Peale that he had saved your life. What do you mean, saved your life?"

" 'Just that,' he said. 'Several years ago I was soloist for the Glen Gray orchestra—when it was one of the greatest in the country. My voice slipped and I finally lost out. I got a job selling. It was very tough for me because it was a terrific comedown in salary. I finally cracked up so badly that I would cry like a baby. Actually, I would cry so much that I often had to pull over to the curb and stop my car and cry. I just couldn't face my prospects. I decided to commit suicide.

" 'But that very day a friend told me about *The Power of*

Positive Thinking. I read it several times. And I got its great idea of limitlessness. I found I could sell as well as I used to sing. Here's my card. I'm now the sales manager of my company. That's why I say Dr. Peale saved my life. And I am so grateful.'"

Again, it was neither I nor my book that saved a life. Actually it was the Creator in the act of re-creating. It was the reactivation of life through the power of faith in God that occurred to both of these people, the taxi driver's wife and the singer. They achieved well-being through a fresh new spiritual outlook. Even more profoundly they were healed by the curative and revitalizing dynamic of faith which God freely offers to any person who wants it badly enough to reach for it.

Just reach for it; but you have really to reach for it. People who go for it get it if they go for it sincerely. There must be real desire, real faith and a sincere reaching out with all your mind and heart for the healing power. This definite inclination of the personality toward the source of power, this comprehensive breaking out of the self which has retreated behind barriers establishes the vital contact over which flows the renewing force of new health.

The process is clearly described in the Bible. "Incline your ear, and come unto me: hear and your soul shall live." (Isaiah 55:3) It is to say, let your whole being lean in God's direction. Turn, really turn to Him. And another instance is the time Jesus healed a man with a withered hand. What a graphic description of a person from whom power and vitality had departed—"a withered hand"—the hand being a symbol of force. Jesus said to him: "Stretch forth thy hand. And he did so: and his hand was restored whole as the other." (Luke 6:10) That is the secret: stretch forth your hand, i.e. reach for it! Really reach for it with all you've got. And even though your personality may be "withered" it will be restored and you will be given new power to live.

That technique stated by Isaiah is also significant: "Incline your ear—hear and your soul shall live." Inclining and hearing; this twin formula points your personality strongly toward God for it means really listening in depth to His Gospel; not letting it bounce superficially off your ear. It means concentrating so intently that God's re-creative power may penetrate beyond the outer ear and superficial attention, deeply into your inner consciousness. Then you are able to tap the deeper flow of health and energy which vastly surges from God toward truly committed people. But it requires the definite inclination of your basic personality to get this result. And a slavish dependence upon pills is hardly necessary when this powerful healing and renewing process is at work in you.

I met a man recently who has been practicing this "reaching and inclining" for many years with good results. It was in Northern Ireland, a lovely land where mists and fog and golden sunshine alternate to make soft green fields and valleys. Its charming and romantic coastline is ramparted by rugged cliffs, not big ones but little rugged cliffs. The town names are so very musical. And most delightful of all are the people, one of whom is Charlie White.

What especially impressed me was the vitality and enthusiasm of this well-known dealer in English china. At first I took Charlie White to be a man much younger than he actually is. When I learned his exact age: eighty-one, I said in genuine astonishment, "Charlie, you're not eighty-one! I can't believe it."

"So what," he laughed, "I don't feel old—I feel young."

"You sure do seem so. What's your secret? Let me in on it."

"I just don't think old thoughts, that's all."

That's quite a remark when you reflect on it. But my curiosity was not satisfied.

"You must have a good doctor to keep a man in such fine shape physically," I remarked.

"Don't have a doctor. . . . Not the kind you mean," he answered. "But actually I have three doctors—and they keep me from getting old or sick by keeping my thinking healthy. Know who they are? Dr. Diet, Dr. Quiet and Dr. Merryman."

Well, those three "doctors" are very good ones indeed. Anyone can benefit from their medication. They are of great help to Doctors of Medicine, too, in their healing work.

Dr. Diet scarcely needs any buildup for the connection between vitality and sensible diet is recognized. By the way, I would like to refer you to a book on sensible eating by my medical doctor brother, Dr. Robert C. Peale. It's entitled: *Live Longer and Better*. It contains a simple workable system that has helped me and many others so I pass it on as a suggestion for you.

Dr. Quiet deserves much emphasis, as does Dr. Merryman. Physicians tell us that a cheerful disposition is a most important factor in good health. The Bible says, "A merry heart doeth good like a medicine: but a broken spirit drieth the bones." (Pr. 17:22)

But let us go deeper in this whole matter of Divine Healing. An old and dear friend of mine was suddenly called upon to face the problem of cancer. I watched admiringly and prayerfully as he dealt with his problem so magnificently and, as it proved, effectively too. I am sure the telling of my friend's experience and the outlining of his method of attack on his problem will help you, as it helped me.

It was well over a year ago that I received from this man news of his illness and discouraging prognosis. He received this blow with the disciplined control that a spiritually conditioned man demonstrates when crises strike. "I am conscious," he said, "of a new hurdle to be dealt with and am aware of the presence of God as never before. It is still as though I am on the edge of that awareness and am now actually beginning to feel His presence."

He shared his problem immediately and completely with his wife. Together they agreed on the course he should take.

Then he went actively to work in a systematic manner to do something constructive about his problem. He did not settle back into self-pity or depression. Certainly he did not give up and abjectly accept this development as the end. He made a strong, well-planned counterattack against the disease, employing, in addition to excellent medical supervision, the powerful spiritual principles in which by long practice he had become well versed.

First he enlisted a team of people whom he knew he could trust to keep his confidence, a spiritual team to work with him and from whom he might draw support in the form of prayer, love, faith and counsel. This team consisted of a few, long-time close spiritual friends; like-minded people of faith. One of the first decisions made by the team was to spare his family knowledge of his condition until the outcome of the battle had been indicated.

Second he determined to use this disease creatively; to make of it a spiritual demonstration of God's grace and power in a specific and difficult situation. This is described in a message he sent me after the healing process had shown considerable progress: "A truly wonderful thing has begun to happen to me; more wonderful even than the disintegration and destruction of the malignant cells with which I was afflicted. I say 'was' because I *am* not afflicted. The dawning of increased sense of awareness makes the wild cells of relatively no consequence. The power of God will take care of and dispose of them when He wills to complete the process. In the meantime, I begin to have a peace and assurance I have never known before." The effect of this man's demonstration upon those of us "on the outside" added immeasurably to our spiritual growth and our own "awareness."

Third he "took spiritual authority" over the wild cells. He proceeded to "direct" the cells of tissue to disintegrate and permit the organ to shrink back to normal size and softness. This unusual procedure was based on the theory that mind controls matter, even within the body and that if you have firm control of your mind and understand the functioning of your body, you can control conditions within the limits of that functioning. So, "I commanded those tissues, through the channel of mind over my nervous system from the brain to yield to the power of God flowing into and through me."

Grounds for such taking of authority over the wild cells to disintegrate in order to permit the diseased organ to normalize are stated in Luke 9:1, where Jesus gave to His disciples "power and authority over all devils and to cure diseases." Surely cancer qualifies as a "devil." And may we not believe that a disciple who is empowered to control devils in other areas of life is also given authority over a devilish thing working within himself! We do not begin to realize the immense power conferred by Christ upon the true believer; upon the completely surrendered person. Therefore it seems in logical harmony with God's laws and with His will also that a present day disciple may take and use the authority given by Christ to His disciples in Bible times. The Master placed no time limitation upon the authority given; nor is there any record of His having withdrawn it. Therefore, this conferral of power still holds good in the twentieth century.

Our friend emphasized that he prayed in the name and in the true spirit of Christ. Always scrupulously honest, he struggled a bit with the question as to whether he was making assumptions that he had no right to make; was he going too far with his faith and was he practically advising God what His decisions should be? However, he felt he had reached a sensible and right reconciliation between the two ideas; namely, the practicing of spiritual authority as conferred upon him and acquiescence to God's will. He assured me, "I do accept His will, praying even as the Master prayed 'Thy will not mine be done.' "

Fourth he emptied from mind, heart and soul any unhealthy attitude or wrong thoughts or erroneous action that might disturb his harmony or right relationship with man or with God.

Fifth he utilized the very best available medical diagnosis and treatment.

Sixth he believed in and faithfully submitted himself to constant treatment by the greatest of all physicians, that Doctor who keeps office in the New Testament. He meticulously applied that therapy on basis of faith as guided by prayerful reading of God's word.

I have given here a rather detailed description of this man's dealing with his problem and of course with his permission, as he and I feel it may be helpful to others in meeting similar crises.

We are for the most part woefully inadequate in our knowledge of God's healing laws and their application to illness. The experience we have related is that of only one man and takes no account of other equally spiritual people who did not achieve healing, but it does trace the steps that led to a positive result in one case. Thus it suggests procedures that may prove valid in the experience of others. This experience may be taken as a spiritual laboratory demonstration and could add to our slowly increasing knowledge of the uses of faith in major illness.

As an active member of my friend's "spiritual team" I have closely followed the course of his dealing with his disease and marvel not only at his scientific-spiritual approach to the problem, but perhaps even more at the amazing control of mind and spirit which he demonstrated. He achieved as complete a victory as I have ever seen over the fear and depression incident to such cases.

I was delighted to read in his latest letter of the thorough physical examination recently made and that the results were negative. The validity of my friend's approach seemed confirmed by the remark of the doctor after the examination: "I am very happy for you. Someone must be praying for you." And of another doctor: "I wonder if our diagnosis was wrong, because there is nothing there." And by the meaningful statement of the patient: "The best part of the entire experience is our closer relationship with God."

So in all crises of life there is always an answer that answers. And that answer is to be found in the application of the spiritual procedures outlined for our guidance and help.

Sum-up of *Feel Healthy without Slavish Dependence upon Pills*

1. Medication is of course important but do not conclude that a pill dissolving in your stomach is necessarily more powerful than a healing thought dissolving in your mind.

2. God's peace deeply imbedded in your mind can often have a more tranquilizing and healing effect upon nerves and tension than medicine. God's peace is itself medicinal.

3. Practice living with Christ in your mind. Daily saturate your consciousness with thoughts of Him. Repeat His words committing them to memory. Think of Him as your real and constant companion.

4. Let the certain faith grow in you that Jesus Christ is here present today no less than in Bible times.

5. Remind yourself that healing of the fear of sickness and death is even more important than physical restoration; that the control of such fear is vital to the healing of the body.

6. Cultivate will power, that massive creative force that God the creator built into you. Do not let it remain flabby but strengthen it by use and exercise.

7. Remember you can make yourself sick or well by the

habitual thoughts you think. Don't drain back into your body the diseased thoughts of your mind.

8. Reach, really reach for the blessing of health which God offers you.

9. Emphasize God's amazing limitlessness within your own life.

10. Never allow sick attitudes to poison your thinking, nor let ill will make you ill. Remember that ill will is sick will. Avoid making your mind "sore" by that painful rehurting called resentment.

EIGHT

TACKLE PROBLEMS HOPEFULLY AND HANDLE THEM CREATIVELY

A roaring blizzard hit St. Louis that March morning. Winter, supposedly dying, lashed out with full fury in one of those early spring storms that piles snow waist-high and sends the thermometer tumbling.

I had intended flying to Kansas City and Wichita but all planes were grounded, so I proceeded to the Union Station to take a Missouri Pacific train. The taxi cab slid over the icy streets, and the heavy snow, piling up on the windshield, blocked the driver's vision. "Bad morning," he growled.

At the station the porter carrying my bags grumbled, "Sure is a bad morning." Under the train sheds the wind surged and sighed like a lost soul. Ice made walking on the platforms treacherous. The wind, catching up huge scoops of snow from atop the drifts, sprinkled it on our faces and down our necks. Everyone plodding morosely along confided to everyone else that it was "a bad morning." The consensus was—a bad morning!

About to enter my car I heard my name called and turned to see a man coming along. He motioned to me to wait. He was a heavy-set fellow who wore no overcoat or hat. His jacket, swinging open, revealed a physique of ample proportion. His face was ruddy with the cold and his fairly sparse hair was mussed by the wintery breeze. A big smile wreathed his face as he boomed out in a voice that must have been trained calling hogs on the prairies, "Hello, Doctor, how do you like this? Isn't it a glorious bad morning?"

Slapping me a terrific whack on the back he passed to the car ahead leaving in his wake the first smiles I'd seen that day. In my seat I found myself repeating that curious phrase, "A glorious bad morning." I realized that the man who spoke it had something, some up-beat quality. He emanated vitality, life, optimism. I decided to see what made him tick, as they say, and went in search of him. I found him regaling several people with stories that had them all laughing. This one man was refurbishing the atmosphere for everyone.

I finally pried him loose from his audience and we got to talking which, incidentally, wasn't difficult. He liked to talk and I'm no slouch at it myself. "Tell me something," I asked. "That phrase—glorious bad morning—where in the world did you get it?"

"Where do you think?" was his quick answer. "You ought to know. I got it from God."

"Go on . . ." I urged, "how, why, when, and where?"

"I claim to have been the worst negative thinker this side of the Rocky Mountains. I was pessimist number one. I could tell you in detail what was wrong with the country and the world and everybody in it. I was loaded down with problems. They were riding me hard. I was plain miserable."

"Then what happened?" I asked. I saw that here was a sharp, keen-minded man who was nobody's fool. He had that thing called personality force. He was a somebody. And he was a tough-minded optimist.

"It's very simple—no mystery to it. I got religion. My life

was changed. You see, my son who loved me despite my being a sour old apple, started telling me about the new preacher at the church. No preacher had ever got to me since I was a boy. We had a couple back there who had something but I'd quit going to church long since. It left me cold. Maybe it was my fault. Perhaps I was unreachable. I don't know.

"But I could see that my son, Fred, was sold on this young preacher. And it seemed that something had come over him; he was happier and more on the ball than ever before, so I dragged along to church one Sunday. And he was right— this preacher did have something. He stood up there and talked without any of that preacher-talk. He talked plain U.S. English. I knew what he was talking about, too. But beyond all that the man showed happiness and peace of mind.

"He was a real salesman, too, for he called on me the next day in my office. He just put his feet up and talked. And I liked him. In fact, I called him up and took him to lunch a couple of days later. He never said a word about religion or anything. I now see he was simply exposing his spiritual merchandise. He knew how to sell a tough customer. Well, to make a long story short he led me to Christ and before I knew it I was right smack in the Kingdom."

He stopped talking and looked at me and he had a look on his face that almost brought tears to my eyes. He was, for a fact, in the Kingdom. And I felt closer to it myself just being exposed to this man.

"Well," he continued, "all that old gloom passed off just like snow melts when the spring sun goes to work on it. Before all this happened, problems wore me out. But now I like 'em; I actually like 'em, believe it or not. Oh, don't think there aren't some rough spots but somehow we get over them better than before."

Back in my own seat I looked out over an absolutely white landscape. The sun struggled through clouds which presently cleared away. Drifts almost covered the fences and each post carried a big white snow cap. Dazzling sunlight reflected myriads of diamonds. Even the train rolled extra quietly through the heavy-padded whiteness of the sun-kissed snowy prairies. It was for a fact "a glorious bad morning."

In the days following I found myself thinking more and more of the powerful effect of optimism upon human beings. In fact, I made an intensive study of it to determine what it contributes and the methods by which it may be cultivated. Moreover, I deliberately practiced it myself and discovered anew that a regular systematic practice of optimism is important in fixing it firmly in the consciousness. My friend on the train derived his optimistic attitude toward problems from a dramatic change in his thinking but even so a daily practice of his new attitude had contributed to his expertness in this vitalized way of thinking and acting.

Optimism is positive thinking lighted up. Some chronic objectors to anything that smacks of hopefulness have decried positive thinking as an overly bright view of life and a kind of jaunty disregard of pain and trouble in this world. Some people have distorted my emphasis, often deliberately, I have felt. Others simply have misunderstood.

The positive thinker is a hard-headed, tough-minded and factual realist. He sees all the difficulties, and I mean all, and what's more he sees them clearly . . . which is more than can be said for the average negative thinker. The latter invariably sees everything in shadowy discoloration. But the positive thinker, unlike the negativist, does not allow difficulties and problems to depress him, and certainly not to defeat him. He looks expectantly beyond all acknowledged difficulties for creative solutions. In other words, he sees more than difficulties—he tries to see the solutions of those difficulties.

The positive thinker has a longer and more penetrative insight. He is completely objective. He has definitive goals. He never takes no for an answer. He is, in short, indomitable; not the kind that will take a licking. He just keeps on fighting and thinking and praying and working and believing and you'd be surprised how many times the positive thinker comes out of the toughest and seemingly most hopeless situations with positive results. And, even if he doesn't, he has the satisfaction of knowing he gave it a good try, which is something, a mighty satisfying something. And maybe, just maybe, the positive thinker who didn't win his objective won something even more precious: his own manhood—his own soul.

So, I decided to write this chapter on hopefulness. Actually this chapter is what the doctor ordered. A thoughtful physician once told me, "If you want to contribute to the public health, I suggest you speak and write often on the necessity for hopefulness, optimism and expectancy. Put some real upbeat into people's minds." He explained how important is a happy and optimistic spirit in healing, and went so far as to say that pessimism in a patient reduces the natural healing processes by ten per cent. I asked how he could pinpoint a particular percentage figure and found him vague on this; but the idea is that when your mind is filled with optimism your natural re-creative forces are stimulated.

Another physician, in reviewing his practice of some forty years, said that many patients would not have been ill and forced to consult him if they had simply practiced optimism, faith and joy. He said, "Quite apart from medication, if I can get them to lift themselves mentally for ten minutes every day into an area of pure joy—meaning undiluted optimism, I can get them well and keep them well." So it seems that medically, also, optimism is important.

Again and again in the Bible references are made to joy, faith, optimism. "These things," Jesus said, "have I spoken unto you, that my joy might remain in you, and that your joy might be full." (John 15:11) Take optimism, therefore, as medicine for the body, mind and soul. Optimism is based on faith, hope and expectation; and there is therapeutic value in the mere act of hoping. The Bible recognizes this also in a moving passage: "Why art thou cast down, O my soul? and why art thou disquieted within me? hope thou in God; for I shall yet praise Him who is the health of my countenance, and my God." (Ps. 42:11) It is to say that if you have hope in God and expectation, it will show on your face as health and vitality.

And so the tough-minded optimist has the ability to see possibilities in everything, however dark. The fact is that most of us do not look for possibilities. By some unhappy quirk of human nature we are inclined to look for difficulties rather than possibilities. And this may be just why difficulties take precedence over possibilities in our lives.

I once knew a man who called himself a "possibilitarian" —meaning one who sees the possibilities rather than the impossibilities. "Well . . . well . . . let's just see what possibilities there are in this situation" he would say sort of drawling-like while others sat around taking dismal views. It was amazing how often he found possibilities too, and then the gloom artists would wonder why they hadn't seen them. The answer was that the possibilitarian was always looking for possibilities, and they never were. You usually find just about what you really look for.

This possibilitarian was a dauntless man, rugged, wise and urbane. You just couldn't phase him with problems no matter how high you piled them. You got the impression that actually he rather enjoyed problems of all kinds, that life for him would be dull without them. He never seemed to have more pleasure than when he went into action against a tough problem. He really enjoyed it. He was quite a man, to say the least. Knowing him was one of my greatest experiences in life.

He was wise, too, and I knew where he got much of his wisdom. It came straight out of the Holy Bible. He knew the Bible from cover to cover. He lived with its characters. Indeed they were like living people to him. He wrote the most unusual and striking comments in the margins of page after page of his Bible. Alongside the story of a man who sinned greatly, and who was given a rough time because of his sins, he wrote "Ha, ha, he sure got what was coming to him!" Yet a kindlier or more helpful man never lived.

I recall one time I had a problem that really had me stopped. I couldn't see a ray of light and, believe me, I was discouraged. So I went to talk it over with the possibilitarian.

He said "All right, son, let's lay that problem of yours out here on the table. Let's just walk around it mentally and prayerfully and see what we can see." Then he walked around the table poking his finger as though prodding the problem on all sides. He had arthritis in his fingers and the joint of his right index finger was noticeably enlarged. The finger was curved but he could point straighter with that crooked finger than most people with a straight one. "I never saw a problem that didn't have a soft spot somewhere if you just keep on poking," he muttered.

Presently he found the "soft" point and started to worry it like a dog with a bone. Finally, he began to chuckle, "Here it is, son. I think we've found the soft spot in your problem. Let's just break it open and see what we can do with it." And he did a lot with it!

Even for him answers didn't always come easily, but the main thing is they did come. Believe me, I learned a lot from my old friend, the possibilitarian, and the chief thing I learned is that there are always possibilities where there seem to be none at all. That's what it is to be a tough-minded optimist. Just keep on poking.

I feel sorry sometimes for young people in this lackluster

day and age. I grew up when it was in the American tradition to believe in boundless progress. There was dynamic hope in the days ahead. We believed the future was all before us. Now young people seem to be trained in the idea that the world is in a perfectly awful shape and we are lucky if we can just survive it at all. This is the gloomy sophisticated attitude of much so-called scholarship. At least I get that notion from some doleful eggheads. To be a scholar it appears appropriate to wear a sour look on your face and carry a dismal attitude in your mind.

One day in San Francisco walking along California Street on Nob Hill I met an intellectual. How did I know he was an intellectual? He told me that he was. Had he not told me I wouldn't have had the slightest idea. But he was dressed as an intellectual is supposed to turn himself out. He had on a black jersey and his shirt was open three buttons down to expose what was presumed to be a manly chest, but which actually looked rather pinched to me. His trousers hadn't been pressed in a long time and his shoes, originally white, looked deliberately beat up—from which I concluded he was a beatnik and probably lived in a garage. He had that dismal, bored look, and he said to me, in a tone that belied the fact, "I am glad to meet you."

I asked the Lord to forgive me and answered that I was glad to meet him also. "You're that super-happy fellow who runs around the country talking about that bright and fortuitous positive thinking, aren't you?" he asked rudely.

"Well," I said, "you are correct in some of your assumptions and erroneous in others. I do run around the country and I do talk about positive thinking which is bright, all right, but not fortuitous. Moreover, it is for men, and . . ." I added more maliciously than I should have, "that is why some people don't comprehend it."

The super-concerned so-called scholarly look deepened and

he said, "But don't you know that the world is full of trouble and problems?"

"I know it is full of trouble and I'm quite aware of the problems. Do you think I was born yesterday? I could tell you something about problems that you, in your pained withdrawal from the world, never heard of. I recognize the problems. But thanks be to God, the world is also full of the overcoming of trouble and the solving of problems."

He had no retort for that and went off down the street shaking his head and I could almost hear it rattle all the way down the block.

This man had taken on the angry and bored way of viewing life which is seemingly the style among the mixed-up. No doubt he is a nice enough fellow if he would shake off that dyspeptic and choleric attitude toward the world. Of course, life is full of trouble and, of course, it is full of problems; but mark this fact: it is also full of the overcoming of trouble and it is also full of the solving of problems. And if we don't overcome and solve where does that leave us?

There is nothing in this life quite so satisfying as to surmount trouble, and nothing so exciting as to take apart a hard tough problem and put it together rightly. And this can be done, even pleasurably done, when your mind is conditioned by a working optimism and faith and to that add expectancy.

And you can condition your mind to be of that tough-minded optimistic quality by employing the creative, scientific and spiritual techniques described in this book.

In making optimism effective an important element is to achieve a state of harmony. The individual who is in harmony within himself and with others is to that degree effective. When you are not in such harmony you are to that degree ineffective. As stresses are reduced or better still eliminated harmonious efficiency will begin to show in your think-ing and performance.

I once spoke to a convention of machinery manufacturers one of whom told me that a basic factor in making a machine effective is the degree to which stress is removed permitting its component parts to work harmoniously together. "When the machine works harmoniously in all its parts," he said, "it actu-ally seems to sing for joy. Then its efficiency quotient is high."

If that is true of a machine certainly it can be no less true of a human being. When you are agitated by conflicts and stresses and confusion, your personality which is designed as a working unity of body, mind and spirit cannot function efficiently. The corrective of harmony is required.

A coach for big league baseball clubs and tennis instructor told me how he always emphasized the importance of joy and harmony in championship athletics. He had a girl pupil who technically was one of the best tennis players he had ever trained but only from the standpoint of technique. There was no deeper harmonious flow in the girl's game and despite technical perfection her work failed to measure up to the highest potential. One day he stopped by the net and sur-prisingly asked, "Do you know the Blue Danube Waltz? Enough so you could hum it with me?" She was surprised but said she thought she could. "All right," he said, "as we play tennis I want you to time your strokes to the harmony of the Blue Danube Waltz."

She thought this a rather strange procedure but complied, and as she entered into the music she was amazed how her strokes began to increase in grace, symmetry and harmony. After the lesson she came to him face aglow, "I never felt be-fore the joy and power of this game. I got into the swing of it really for the first time in my life." Subsequently she be-came a star performer; she developed the true flow of har-mony.

Actually, the game of life is little different. When you fight the game, or fight the job, or fight life you are under stress and therefore you build up resistance simply because you are out of harmony. So naturally optimism declines. But when your mind is full of joy, when you love whatever you are doing—whether selling groceries, writing books, raising children, practicing law or medicine, or going to school—when you love it and are full of happiness about it, then you step up your harmony and there is a flow to your thinking, to your living and working which makes it truly enjoyable. Result? You become much more effective. So start developing both inner and outer harmony for if you are on the outs either with yourself or others then actually you are as they say "out of it."

I am aware that my emphasis on optimism no matter how tough-minded is hard for some people to take. As a matter of fact it even seems to irk some of the more critical because basically they hate to see anything go well; it actually bothers them. You would think they would be happy about it. But no, instead they seem to resent any and all hopeful signs. If things weren't bad they would have nothing to be sad and gripey about.

Probably the reason for such hostile reaction to success by some is an unconscious recognition that they themselves aren't doing so well; so it follows, in warped logic, that they don't want anyone else, or even society itself, to do well. Of course, they deny this and cloud their neurotic will to fail behind a barrage of big humanitarian, social-concern words strung together in what they assume to be a scholarly fashion. In fact, the more erudite and egg-head-like the expression of gloomy negativism the more certain you can be that this pessimism takes its rise from deep-seated inner frustration and sense of failure. You need not be a psychologist to note that transparently clear fact about some of our ultra academically conditioned gripers.

The unhealthy mess of sour thinking works itself out in the current style of what Dr. Henry M. Wriston, former president of Brown University, calls "self-flagellation." "We're in a self-flagellating mood today," he wrote in an article in *Think* magazine. "We like to beat ourselves. I'm sick of it. Our motto seems to be; anything you can do we can do worse. This is the first continental democracy in the world and from much current criticism you'd think it was a flop. Hell no, it isn't."

How right Dr. Wriston is! Of course, everything isn't sweetness and light, nor a bed of roses. Whoever said that it was? But neither is everything necessarily going to pot. It's somewhere in between those extremes but we had better believe in progress and pray for it and work for it or we will surely sink just as low as some of the dismal croakers hope that we will. No matter how low we do sink they wouldn't be satisfied. Their sadistic natures would still require the hair shirt of self-flagellation. The egg-head, self-flagellators are the true pillar saints of our time though it bores them to be compared to anything pertaining to religion from which they claim complete emancipation. Actually they have never been emancipated from anything, particularly from themselves, being everlastingly pushed around by the persistent irritant of never quite finding themselves.

It's a curious generation that is always asking questions and never getting answers. It is just full-up with saddish people who are always trying to find themselves but somehow never do. So, failing to get organized, they take recourse in disorganization. They grow whiskers and pessimism and sit around with sad looks in grubby taverns swilling beer in a bored sort of way. They act so very tough that you know they aren't tough at all. Under most of the whiskers I see on our bored, sad, angry young men is an ill disguised baby boy look around the mouth. And so they go along year after year always painfully trying to find themselves, asking, ever asking questions, looking for answers they don't find.

Did you ever notice the arrogantly self-conscious attitude of the whisker wearers? Anyone who has ever been bothered by an inferiority complex, as I have been, actually is made, despite himself, to feel halfway uncomfortable, and hopelessly antiquated because he isn't decked out in whiskers too. That could be why some take it up.

But let's face it, you can't hide an inferiority complex behind a bush of hair on your face. Now please don't get the idea this book is a big crusade against whiskers. On some men, grown up men that is, a beard is actually in keeping, even impressive. But the point is you have to be a man to wear whiskers well. Only a man who has at least found himself has what it takes to get away with whiskers.

Of course not all of the doubters about optimism are of the beatnik variety. There are not a few normal everyday hardworking, hard-thinking people and scholars who are seriously concerned about many issues and to them hopefulness seems unrealistic, even superficial. And for them and their concern I have respect. But the tough-minded optimist has the soundest attitude; he sees all the evils and sees them straight but he still believes in better outcomes than appear likely at the moment.

Only recently on a plane I encountered a man who in current jargon expressed what might be construed as a dim view of life. In fact, as he regaled me with his ideas I found myself recalling Schopenhauer's: "Optimism cuts a sorry figure in this theatre of sin, suffering and death."

This person's approach was, you might say, slightly lacking in what used to be called elegance. Bristling with aggressiveness which verged on hostility toward the whole world, and using theological words which were hardly put together in a theological manner, he wanted to know "where in the h___" I got this positive thinking stuff. Didn't I know the world was in a terrible mess? So what did I mean positive thinking! . . . et cetera ad infinitum.

When he finally ran down because he ran out of words—having indicated by his facile resort to dull profanity a paucity of descriptive vocabulary—I averred that I hadn't picked up my philosophy in hell, as he seemed to believe, and that I would stack it solidly up against his "sappy" pessimism anytime, anywhere; so what did he think about that?

Thus we squared off with no holds barred, and grinned friendly like at each other. I told him that as a positive thinker I had more downright guts than he did as a negative thinker, for positive thinkers take a straight, hard look at the seamy side, but they don't let it throw them. They don't moan and give up, but get busy, with God's help, to do something about the world's problems. I asked him why he didn't get on that beam too and be more than just a loud but soft-minded talker.

I suggested we take a look together at these tough problems, and I read from an editorial in *The Church Herald* of my own denomination, the Reformed Church in America. This article I felt was a true Christian statement that faced facts and was not abashed or frightened by them. The real Christian mind is by all odds the toughest mind in the world. It sees things exactly as they are, but doesn't stop there. It also sees things as, by God's grace and our intelligence, they can become.

Let me quote from the statement which I read to my problem-swamped traveling companion:

> There are many signs that we are witnessing the waning influence of Christianity on our continent. The predominant philosophy in higher education is naturalism, which is just as atheistic as atheistic communism. The

Bible is slowly being forced out of the public schools. Our crime rate stands at an all-time high. Sub-Christian morals blare out at us from almost every newsstand. Most of the 'best-sellers' in books and magazines are non-Christian if not anti-Christian in morals and message. You would never guess from the television shows or the life they depict that over 50 per cent of the people in the United States are affiliated with some Christian church. Materialism, the worship of things even while we profess with our lips to believe in God, seems to be on the ascendancy everywhere. Moral standards are slipping back to what they were before Jesus Christ came into this world. Too much of our life goes on just as though He never lived or died, or rose again.

We citizens of the United States spend more money on liquor than on education. More of our children become bartenders than ministers of the Gospel. Great masses of so-called Christian people seldom, if ever, attend church services and live practically without God. Many of them seem to be more interested in sex appeal than in saintliness. Fornication is called fun, and lust goes by the name of love. No wonder we have broken homes—juvenile delinquency. We have, in the words of Jeremiah, 'committed two evils: we have forsaken God, the fountain of living waters, and hewed out cisterns for ourselves, broken cisterns, that can hold no water.' It is such a time as Jesus foretold when He said 'Because wickedness is multiplied most men's love will grow cold.'

We confess Jesus Christ is the Lord, but His will is far from dominant in this world which is in rebellion against God. His Gospel, maligned and opposed from the beginning, probably faces a greater variety of subtle, entrenched and demonic opposition today than ever before in its history. Most ominous and diabolical of all is atheistic communism, with its tyrannical hold upon some 900,000,000 people over one-third of the earth's population, attained within one short generation.

This picture may seem to be pure pessimism but these facts cannot be disputed. We had better see things as they really are, in true perspective for there is nothing more dangerous than illusion. But if there are only 300 of us left, we had better know it. Knowing it may help us to quit our trust in gimmicks and put our trust in God alone, to depend not upon men and their methods, but upon the Lord and His Gospel. Of our present situation also Jesus would surely say, 'What is impossible with men is possible with God'.

If ours is in a sense a day of decadence and defeat, it is nevertheless also at the same time a day of opportunity. Mighty as communism and certain pagan religions seem today, God is still stronger than Satan. 'Behold, the Lord's hand is not shortened, that it cannot save, nor His ear dull, that it cannot hear.' We may not see victory today, but we can work, and fight, and pray, and hope, because we believe in Jesus Christ.

So concluded this editorial which certainly laid it on the line.

As we zoomed through the sky at some 500 miles per hour considering the above my seat mate commented, "Well, if the church has even a few tough men of faith such as that editorial represents, then it could be that I'm all wet. O.K. . . . I'll try to go for the idea that there is an answer to the mess we are in." (But he didn't altogether step out of character.) "Let's try making something out of this lousy world." Now he was talking with an upbeat. He will find, if he really works with this kind of thinking, that optimistic undefeatable faith in God does produce creative results regardless of how tough things are.

The indisputable fact that life is hard and beset by problems does not depreciate the value of the hopeful outlook nor the creative approach. If everything were bright and fortuitous, the poignant joy of improvement would be less for then it would, of course, be commonplace. It is in the sharp contrast of joy with pain that life's deepest satisfactions are to be found. Therefore, in urging the attitude that we can handle problems we do not close our eyes to pain and trouble, but on the contrary, we advocate the quest for creativity within the pattern of difficulty. And, indeed, any other course would scarcely be possible since that is where it must be found.

There seems to be current a strange notion that the fact of hard, tough problems rules out hopefulness: that simply because we have problems a pessimistic attitude is called for.

In fact, this notion is expressed in not a few hundreds of letters that come to me from my readers. Now, of course, I realize full well that problems can be, and often are, unpleasant and pesky in the extreme. And they do add to the difficulty of living. There is no doubt about that. But that their existence and demanding presence should subtract optimism just does not follow. Indeed, their absence would indicate that the ultimate in pessimism had arrived for no problems would mean, literally, no life. And only with life is creative achievement possible.

Let me illustrate this point. I was walking down Fifth Avenue recently when I encountered a friend named George. It was quite evident that he wasn't what you would describe as effervescently happy. Indeed he wore a most disconsolate and woebegone expression on his countenance, which excited my natural sympathies so I asked him, "How are you, George?"

Now, when you get right down to it, this was simply a routine inquiry but George took it seriously and proceeded in meticulous detail to enlighten me on the subject of how badly he felt. Fifteen minutes later he was still dealing with the subject, though I had long since been convinced that he was in a despondent frame of mind, with accompanying ill feelings.

"Well, George," I said sympathetically, "I am sorry that you see your situation so darkly and feel so badly." (Incidentally, that kind of seeing and that result in feeling go together like Siamese twins.) "I would like to be of some help to you. I'm certainly on your team and will do anything I can for you."

"If you could only get me loose from this mess of problems that is making my life miserable. Problems, problems, and more problems—that's all I have, and I am sick of it. I'm fed up with problems." He threw up his hands in a gesture of futility and despair.

"Tell you what, Norman," he growled. "If you will help me get rid of these problems, I'll give you one thousand dollars cash for your work." Well, I am not one to turn down an offer like that, and I tried to cooperate with George.

"O.K. George," I said. "I think I can help you, at least with a thought. I was at a place the other day not very far from here where there are one hundred thousand people and not a single one of them has a problem."

"Boy, that's for me," responded George showing the first glimmer of optimism I'd yet detected in him. "That sure is for me. Where is this place? Lead me to it!"

"Well, if you really want to know," I said, "it's Woodlawn Cemetery in the Bronx. There are no problems there—none at all. But the trouble is that everyone in Woodlawn is dead. So, George," I continued, "don't be too sorry that you have those problems, for actually they are a sign of life; they prove that you aren't dead."

And, of course, that is exactly what problems are: the indication of participation, which itself indicates vitality and existence. In fact, it follows that the person who has fifty problems is twice as alive as the individual who has only twenty-five. And if by some strange chance you have no problems at all, you had better get right down on your knees and pray to the Lord asking: "Lord, what's the matter? Don't you trust me any more? Please give me some problems."

So be glad—yes, actually be glad that you have problems. Be grateful for them as implying that God has confidence in your ability to handle these problems with which He has entrusted you. Adopt this attitude toward problems and it will tend to siphon off the depression you may have developed from a negative reaction toward them. And as you develop the habit of thinking in hopeful terms about your problems, you will find yourself doing much better with them.

This will add to your enjoyment of life too for one of the few greatest satisfactions of this life is to handle problems efficiently and well. Moreover this successful handling tends to build up your faith that, through God's help and guidance, you have what it takes to deal with anything that may ever face you.

What a strange and sad notion is the concept that has gained currency in recent years that humanitarian progress is achieved by relieving people of problems rather than by making them self-reliantly able to handle problems. Such tender-heartedness sounds well when wept over in the pulpit or by a politician running for election but the plain fact remains that people are never truly helped or even genuinely loved unless they are led to find strength and know-how to do for themselves. When that is proven to be impossible then naturally they should be cared for by others, but only then.

But still the idea persists among the super-tenderhearted, even bleeding-hearted, that problems are just terrible things and the world should be rid of them. The method for so doing is, of course, via starry-eyed legislation in Washington. One wonders whether the politicians, who are always actually less starry-eyed and more cynically aware of the main chance than they profess, have not found this mechanism a glorious device for raking in the votes; and corralling votes is, of course, their main purpose in living.

Strong men, creative men, men who do things do not hate problems at all—in fact, they like them. They know that problems are to the mind what exercise is to the muscles, they toughen and make strong. Problems make one better able to cope with life.

One of the men I've admired most was the late famous Charles F. "Boss" Kettering, scientific genius of General Motors. He created the self-starter, Duco paint process for automobiles and many other modern devices. He was one of the most stimulating thinkers I ever knew.

At a dinner in Cleveland to celebrate the 150th Anniversary of Ohio's admission to the Union as a state, a number of native Ohioans had been invited to speak. On the program were Branch Rickey, Dr. Milliken, Bob Hope, myself and others.

The toastmaster departed from the program and called on "Boss" Kettering who was sitting in the audience. He came forward and made a two-sentence speech which shall ever remain in my memory as a masterpiece. Referring to the emphasis upon history for which the dinner was being held Kettering said, "I am not interested in the past. I am interested only in the future for there is where I expect to spend the rest of my life." And with that he sat down amidst thunderous applause.

To his aides at General Motors Kettering often said, "Problems are the price of progress. Don't bring me anything but trouble. Good news weakens me." What a philosophy! Bring me problems, they strengthen me. Problems viewed as opportunities make men strong.

The big question isn't whether we have problems and that some of them are extremely difficult and that all of them add to the complications of living. The big thing is your attitude toward problems. How you think of the problem is more important than the problem itself. Menninger says, "Attitudes are more important than facts." Sure a fact is a fact. Some people say that as something final; there's that great big hard fact. So what can you do about it? So they give up.

But the tough-minded optimist takes a positive attitude toward the fact. He sees it realistically, just as it is, but he sees something more. He views it as a challenge to his intelligence, to his ingenuity and faith. He prays and asks for insight and guidance in dealing with the hard fact. He keeps on thinking; he keeps on praying and believing. He knows there is an answer and so finally he finds it. Perhaps he changes the fact or maybe he just by-passes it or perhaps he learns to live with it. But in any case his attitude toward the fact has proved more important than the fact itself.

Practice hopefulness until you master it. Then keep on practicing it, so that you keep it always working. You don't need to take a final licking at any time, ever. With God's help you can handle any problem.

NINE

PRAY YOUR WAY
THROUGH DIFFICULTY

Was she mad! I never saw an angrier woman in all my life. She stormed and I mean stormed in a tirade that just about topped in emotional violence anything I'd ever seen. She had come to talk with me or, more accurately, at me. I could scarcely get a word in edgewise.

She had just discovered that her husband was having an affair with another woman. She and her husband, she kept repeating, had been married for twenty years. He just couldn't do this to her. She had trusted him; thought of course all was O.K. between them; and now this! She couldn't find words strong enough for what she thought of him. He was, it seemed, a two-faced, double-dealing, double-crossing heel of the lowest type.

Naturally, I couldn't condone the husband's conduct but so vindictive and self-righteous was this woman's attitude that actually it explained a lot and I could not help feeling some sympathy for the man.

I thought she would run down, presently, and so I listened sympathetically and quietly, but when she started a second round of the same tirade I called a halt. In counseling I have noted a tendency in upset people endlessly to repeat themselves. One time over a story is sufficient. But try as I would I could not shut off the flow of this lady's vituperation.

So I prayed for guidance. I'm not smart enough to know how to handle such cases on my own, so I asked for direction and got it, too. A dramatic method came to me and it proved effective.

Interrupting her I said, "Now look, we're getting exactly nowhere with this matter. So I suggest we let go completely of the whole problem for a while. Drop it in my hands." I rose, cupped my hands and held them out to her. As though taking her problem into my cupped hands I said, "I've got your problem now." I walked to the door and pushing it open made the gesture of tossing something into the adjoining room and shut the door. "Now your problem is outside. Let's leave it there and start thinking about God instead of the problem." She started to say something. "Please, you've had your say. Keep absolutely silent and so will I. Just sit and think about God until I tell you to stop and I'll do the same."

She was so surprised by this unexpected procedure that she did indeed remain absolutely quiet. I hardly expected that she could, but I was to discover later that she possessed more self-discipline than showed on the surface. After three minutes of silence I took up the Bible and read a few passages selected with a view to emphasizing the Lord's presence. Others I chose for their power to quiet the mind and permit rational mental activity.

Then I said, "You may speak now. What thoughts came to you during that quiet period?"

She hesitated and when the words came they were calm and controlled. The heat was definitely gone. She spoke slowly and intelligently. Now she was no longer a complete victim of emotion; she was now doing some thinking. It was a sort of soliloquy to which I had the honor to listen. I say honor for this was a real person talking. "Well, in spite of everything,

Harry is a fine man. I must think of all his goodness and patience. This isn't really Harry who's got mixed up in this affair." She paused and finally came out with, "Maybe the failure is mine more than his. I must have failed him. I wasn't thinking." How right she was. Many a wife would be spared this kind of thing if only she would think—and not about herself either, but about her husband.

But as much as I respect the power of thought-inducing prayer, I was hardly prepared for her next statement. That it came hard was evident, but that it was expressed at all showed an important grasp of life.

"That poor woman. Look at the sorrow and pain she is bringing upon herself and her family. I hope I can pray that she will find herself." But she was no softie, that's for sure, for suddenly she rose and said, "I'm all right now. I know what to do about myself and I'm sure I can handle the situation." As I watched her go I somehow felt that she could, too, for she had experienced one of the subtlest of all human skills —how to pray her way through difficulty. She, herself had to solve her problem, with God's help. And this she realized.

I have since used this technique in many other problems and in most of them it has proved effective. This particular method involves several factors: the first is a complete emptying of the emotional content. This lady really poured it out. Fortunately I was able to arrest her emotional emptying at just the precise moment and prevent her from building it up again. This is a reason for failure in many such cases; the emotion is emptied then immediately refilled. An endless circle is thus created which results in no constructive ending.

A second factor is that she exorcised or emptied the emotion to another person. I was able to help her by listening respectfully, with esteem for her personality which was at the moment sorely wounded and rejected. By showing esteem I helped restore her ego.

A third factor and one of great importance is that by insisting upon a quiet time, we broke the strain, diverted an otherwise endless circle, and injected a new possibility, that of a guidance beyond herself. When she came to my office she was not in a mood that made thinking possible. But a new mood was created in which thought processes could not only be resumed but on a higher level of insight. By temporarily dropping the problem, in effect bypassing it and diverting to a train of spiritual thought, her mind was freed of stultifying tension and so she relaxed. She was then at once able to produce constructive ideas. In this manner she recovered herself and the ability to handle her problem.

Another person who found this method to be effective runs a large business. He told me that he was once faced with a problem so worrisome that he struggled with it day and night. It rested so heavily upon his mind that he couldn't sleep. He grew tense, irritable, nervous. The more he wrestled with it, the more complex and hopeless the problem seemed. Actually, as he tightened up mentally he was squeezing off the answer and solution.

Pacing his office, he chanced to pause in front of his mother's picture. She had been a simple country woman whom he had not only loved and revered but had greatly admired too for her sharp practical intelligence. As he gazed upon his mother's face, he remembered something he had heard her say many times in perplexing family situations: "Let's just let the problem rest awhile and think about God."

This thought seemed to be a direct message to him in his present situation. So, he removed all the papers from his desk, shoved them into a drawer and pushed it shut. He said to himself, "Now the decks are clear. I will turn away from this problem for a while." From another drawer he took out his Bible, settled back in his chair and started reading in the Book of Psalms. And there, believe it or not, he sat a full half hour, quietly reading the Bible. He turned to some of the passages he knew best, and read the great words aloud. Finally he closed the Bible and sat quite still, thinking about God. He thought about God's goodness; His providence; how vast His mind; how great His love. Then he offered a silent prayer of thanksgiving.

A feeling of calm pervaded his thoughts. His mind grew quiet; his body felt rested. He was relaxed, like a rubber band returning to its natural shape after having been stretched taut.

He returned to work considerably refreshed and stimulated. Suddenly the thought came to go down the street and see a certain man. There was no connection, so far as he could see, between his problem and the man whose name had suddenly occurred to him. But he reasoned that, since the thought had come just after prayer, maybe he better go see the man.

So he went; and in the course of conversation this other man made a seemingly irrelevant remark which, in turn, triggered a thought that burst upon our friend's mind with the force of sudden inspiration. He saw in it, clearly indicated, the first step to a solution of his problem. Subsequent events proved that he had received a real answer.

As a consequence of this experience he now follows the same procedure with any problem posing substantial difficulty. He withdraws attention from the problem long enough to concentrate his faculties upon God. Then he goes back to the problem, but with his mind quieted and relaxed and working at maximum efficiency. As a result, the mind delivers sound insights. He finds this method valid for all kinds of problems. He says it consistently works.

The technique of getting quiet and withdrawing mentally into the presence of God is so very important that it is contrary to all good sense to bypass this method of problem-handling. Some otherwise intelligent people think fuzzily of

God as a kind of remote religious Being solely connected with churches. This is not the great God we know. Some churches have so fenced God around with all sorts of pomp and ceremony that He becomes actually dull and unreal. Of course, God is so much bigger and more fascinating than all this that to thus restrict and reduce Him is a kind of blasphemy, however pious it appears to be.

It used to be assumed that only pastors and perhaps religious laymen urged people to find their answers in God but now it seems that some doctors do just that. For example, a man told me he had for some days felt a decline in energy. He decided he was pushing himself pretty hard so "knocked off" for a two weeks' vacation in Florida. But when he returned "to the old rat race" as he put it, he was as tired as before. "All the time and money spent in Florida went down the drain," he confided. He was the kind of man who resisted going to a doctor and did so only as a last resort. But finally he did consult a physician who gave him a thorough going-over with a complete series of tests. The doctor told him he was suffering from two things, one of which was low blood sugar.

"What do we do about that?" asked the patient who had the satisfying hope that perhaps more intake of sweets would be prescribed. Since he had a well-developed sweet tooth the thought pleased him. But instead, to his surprise, the prescription was "hamburger" for lunch every day until energy returned.

"What's the other thing I'm suffering from, Doc?" he asked. The doctor, a shrewd old practitioner, looked overlong at this hepped-up metropolitan business leader. Thoughtfully, and more to himself than to his patient, he said, "I wonder . . . I just wonder if he has what it takes."

"What do you mean—have I got what it takes?" the man exclaimed with a bit of exasperation.

"Well," said the doctor, "you are low in two things as I see it—blood sugar and spiritual inspiration. So, to the hamburger add, if you will permit me, more of God. God and hamburger," he chuckled, "one to increase the spiritual count; the other to step up the blood sugar."

And that explains how I came into the case. The patient consulted me upon suggestion from the doctor "to get an injection of God." Quite a curious prescription, you might say.

At any rate this patient who "had never gone at all for religion" not only got to going regularly to church, but what is more important, began seriously applying spiritual techniques to himself. As a result he showed definite improvement in nerves and energy. "My new energy really comes," he said, "from the spiritual vitality received when I surrendered my life to God. When I learned to live with God instead of simply trying to keep myself going, I began to live, really live." Which, of course, is another way of saying that he learned to pray his way through difficulty.

But not only physical energy sags. Creative vitality and mental force can get stale as well. The mind which once delivered dynamic ideas and insights can turn into a dry well out of which nothing constructive comes. Under such circumstances prayer has proved to be a powerful reactivating force stimulating and renewing the mind.

For example, I met a man on the street and we walked a few blocks together. I became aware that here was a man who was, you might say, deeply, vibrantly happy.

"I want to tell you," he said, "that the positive thinking program you have been advocating really works. You have no idea what positive prayer has meant to me! It's exciting, believe me."

This man, it seemed, had been having quite a hard time. Everything tended to go wrong, especially in business affairs. He kept "running into stone walls and road blocks," as he put it. His worsening situation left him increasingly frustrated

and discouraged. What bothered him most was that constructive ideas no longer came to him. His mind was a "dry well
—bone dry."

At this juncture he happened to read in one of my newspaper columns about the spiritual and practical technique
which I describe as "taking God as a partner"—a phraseology
new to him but which simply meant putting your life in God's
hands and letting Him run it. I stated in the article that this
simple practice had activated new power, stimulated thinking
and improved performance for many who applied it. My friend
found this article interesting and decided to do the basic
spiritual thinking which it described. He reasoned that he had
tried everything else so he "might as well give this a fling also."

So, as he sat at his desk, he prayed, somewhat as follows:
"Lord, I'll have to admit that I can't seem to handle my situation. I do not seem to get any good ideas anymore. I hate to
admit it but guess I'm just about licked. This business isn't
going well at all. Humbly I ask You to be my senior partner.
I have nothing to offer You except myself. Please change me
and clean up the mess I'm in; and also the mess I am personally. I really do not understand how this can be done and
I may as well tell You frankly, Lord, I have my doubts about
it for it's a new one on me. But I'm ready to do anything You
tell me and will give this partnership a sincere try. Otherwise
I'm in a bad way."

"Did you really say all that in your prayer?" I asked.

"Yes, that's what I said, almost word for word. I wasn't ir-
reverent either."

"Pretty real prayer if you ask me. What happened then?"

"Well," he went on, "after I got through praying I sat back
in my chair and nothing happened. I don't know exactly what
I expected but I had a slight feeling of being let down. And
I thought to myself, well, this is just one of those things. But
then I noticed I was feeling sort of peaceful and easy. I de-

cided to go out and take a walk. I don't know why; it just seemed to be the next thing to do. I walked about a mile and then turned around, thinking I had better get back to the office.

"And on my way back, as I came to the corner of Madison Avenue and 48th Street I suddenly stopped and stood stock still at the curb. Into my mind popped an idea that had not occurred to me before, an idea for solving my main problem. I don't know where it came from. Seemed like it came right out of the blue. But now I know all right where it came from.

"I hurried back to my office and at once started putting the idea into action. It wasn't long until things began to click, one after another, and in a few weeks the whole situation began to look up. I saw light for the first time and other supporting ideas came too. The old brain was on the go again.

"I continued each day putting myself completely into God's hands. Oh, I had some hard days—don't think I didn't. There are still some big difficulties to deal with . . . plenty of them. But for the first time I was making progress from day to day and perhaps what is even more important I felt very different. Do you know, it's sort of funny but when *I* became different everything became different. So, I guess things go about like a fellow is. What do you think?"

"And I'll tell you what I'm doing now," he continued without waiting for a comment, "I am searching through the New Testament every night before going to sleep and making a list of all the things Jesus tells us to do. And I'm really trying to do them. For example, I decided to quit hating anybody. Jesus says to get right with people you've been on the outs with; I have been doing that. He says to have faith; I have been doing that also, or at least trying. I can only say that I have never felt so good and life has never been so exciting."

This man surely did have something. There was no doubt about that. It was evident that he was really alive and had an up-beat spirit. I had known him for years and was astonished at the change in him. He had discovered that prayer is no visionary, pious, mystical exercise for saints and the ultra-devout. He found that it can be a practical method for restimulating the mind which has lost creative skill. And even more than that he found that such praying is an energy-renewing force.

We have already suggested several methods in this chapter for praying your way through difficulty: (1) Deliberately turn from the problem and concentrate on God. Such was the method used in the case of the irate woman whose husband was having an affair and the businessman who was struggling with a perplexing matter. (2) The unique prescription given by the doctor to the businessman who was suffering from depletion of energy. (3) And finally the method used by the man who "took God as a partner."

I now wish to suggest what I call "the write it out and put it in the Bible method." This procedure is based on the principle that much prayer is fuzzy and lacking a clearly defined concept of the problem itself. You have to know what the problem is and be able to outline it in clear and basic detail to get the best results. A solution can hardly be expected if you do not really know what the problem is any more than you can start for and arrive at a destination that has not been decided upon. In other words you have to know what it's all about and where you want to go.

Sometimes you will see in business offices the cryptic directive: *Write it out* or *Put it in a memo*. This directive is designed to eliminate the endless talk, the mussy description, the blurred concept. A first principle in prayer is to know exactly what you want to say, and precisely what objective you have. You must be able to state the problem clearly and succinctly. If you have to use a lot of words that very fact in itself is evidence that you aren't too sure just what is on your mind. A man who thinks his problem through and phrases it so that he himself sees it clearly has thereby made it possible for himself to receive those clear answers which are waiting for him in the mind of God. Only clarity can receive clearly.

So write out your prayer in the fewest possible words. Select each word to convey maximum meaning. Whittle the message down to telegram length. This will tend to clarify your problem.

I designed cards which were placed in the pew racks of the Marble Collegiate Church. Thousands of them have been used to good effect. Even the color of the card was carefully selected as having some possible bearing upon the attitude of the user. It is golden in color to symbolize hope and expectation and reads as follows:

MY PROBLEM(S)

In getting an answer to a problem, it helps to write it. This makes it specific, and you are better able to think it through and pray it through.

Write your problem on this card. Place it in your personal Bible. Pray about it daily. Be willing to accept God's answer.

Finally, note the day the answer comes. Then file the card with thanksgiving.

The reason for suggesting that the card be placed in your personal Bible is to identify your problem with the source Book of wisdom, therefore encouraging you to explore the guidance it offers. Symbolically it is as if you actually placed the problem in the hands of God.

The suggestion to file the card after answers have been re-

ceived, both affirmative and negative, is based on the value of
compiling a history of your relationship with God and His
amazing effect on your life. Such a file of cards will greatly
add to the depth of your faith by documenting the many ways
in which you have been guided and supported spiritually. It
will conclusively show that prayer, properly utilized, is not a
careless hit or miss reaction of desperation or crisis, but a rational working of Divine Law in human affairs.

I could tell many stories of how this card has worked in people's lives but one that is perhaps most interesting is the experience of my wife, Ruth. We each have our own bedside
Bibles in which we read every night and morning. One evening I noticed that, in some way, our Bibles had been shifted
so that Ruth's was on my night table. Out of it dropped a problem card. I realized that the card was private to her but curiosity overcame me and I read it half expecting to find myself
listed as her big problem.

She had written three problems on the card and they were
clearly and succinctly expressed. And she had indicated the
date on which she had done so, January 1, 1960. After problem number one she had written: Answer was "Yes" on _____
1960. After the second problem she had made the notation:
Received a "no" answer on _____ 1960. There was nothing
entered after problem three which indicated that as yet no
answer had been received. I added my prayers to hers and put
the card back into the Bible.

Many weeks, indeed several months later, she got her answer to problem number three. It was "Yes." She showed me
the card the day the glorious "Yes" answer came and then
after problem three, she wrote, "A wonderful 'Yes' answer
today, December 18, 1960, eleven months and eighteen days
after I listed the problem here. Thank you dear Lord."

Then she filed the card and now has gone on to other problems. And of course, that is the way of it; problems are always cropping up. But since this gives us the opportunity to work out more victories and further to experience the goodness of God we should be glad and grateful for problems. Keep on writing out your problems. As you continue to think, pray and believe good answers will come and you will grow thereby and life will become more meaningful and satisfying.

In praying your way through difficulty it is also important to reduce the self-interest element and emphasize the interests of others who may be involved in the problem. I do not mean that a legitimate and normal self-interest is wrong. I mention this because so many who write or speak about prayer assume a super-pious attitude and tell us we should not think of ourselves at all. This is poppycock for the fact is that you are involved in the very nature of life and such extreme depreciation is not possible nor even desirable if it were possible. We are not intended to remove ourselves from life but to live it in right balance. Therefore too much or too little emphasis on self is to be avoided if such balance is to be maintained. When proper balance between self-interest and the interest of others is achieved then spiritual power activates practical results into motion.

An illustration is the experience of H.F., a popular TV personality in the Southwest. I was a guest on his program in an unrehearsed, ad lib discussion in which the conversation touched on various matters. H.F. knows how to achieve a high interest level and his program is amusing and delightful. Finally we got around to the subject of prayer. H.F. said, "Perhaps I don't understand prayer as well as I ought, for sometimes things turn out right and sometimes they don't. Why is that?"

"There are three possible answers to prayer, you know: yes, no, and wait."

"Well," he replied with a grin, "most of the answers I've

been getting are the wait-awhile kind. I have a problem right now."

This discussion was on the air, right out in front of the vast unseen audience of television viewers. And he continued, "Up north I have a house that I must sell. I need the money but just don't know what to do about it. Every day I ask the Lord to help me sell the house at a satisfactory price, but nothing happens. What's wrong? What can I do about it?"

"Perhaps the trouble with your prayer is that you are thinking only of yourself and of how much money you can get for that house," I said. "While Almighty God is of course interested in you, He is interested in others also. Why don't you try to get interested in others also? Perhaps that will get you onto God's wave-length."

He looked blank. "What do you mean?"

"Pray to the Lord something like this: 'Lord, up north I have a nice house which is now empty. Perhaps you know of a family, or maybe a young couple, who are looking for just such a home and who would like my house and be happy living in it. If my house will fit their needs, please bring them to it. And may I meet their need on terms that are reasonable and within their means. Help them and help me, each according to need. I accept Your guidance and I thank You for it.'"

Not long after this incident, I received a letter from H.F. saying:

Dear Dr. Peale:

I am sure you will recall our interview when you were in Houston. I thought you might be interested in knowing that five days after we discussed prayer and positive thinking in relation to selling my house it was sold, and to a family that needed precisely that kind of a house—which was your prayer suggestion.

This is an instance of a problem being solved when a man started thinking of the other fellow and himself in equal balance. Maybe you, I, all of us think too much, even pray excessively in terms of personal welfare.

Sometimes as a matter of fact you just have to think of yourself and, no fooling, for you may be right down to rock bottom or in such extremity that you and your loved ones have just got to have help. The only thing to do in that event is to take it up with the Lord and put the entire problem in His hands. Let it rest there with complete trust. After your prayer for help is answered you will of course gladly share with others to keep the flow of blessings circulating.

In my weekly column which is carried in some two hundred newspapers, I occasionally write about the power of prayer. And I ask my readers to tell me of their own experiences. As you may surmise I have received some fascinating stories of prayer demonstrations in life situations.

One was from Mr. Bean Robinson of El Paso, Texas. I was impressed by his letterhead which reads, "Good Horses, Good Ranches, Good Cattle, Good People. We know them all from Ft. Worth to California, from Chihuahua to Canada."

Mr. Robinson illustrates the truth that God will tell you what to do and when to do it, and that you must listen and do what God says. But read his letter for it is really very interesting.

> Dear Dr. Peale:
> In the El Paso Times, Monday, July 4, you had an article on prayer. You said you would be glad for your friends to write you and tell their experiences so that we might help each other. Prayer to me is like me picking up my telephone and calling God. Now if God is going to help me I have to be able to understand what God tells me. The important thing is, what is God's will for me. I think the perfect prayer would be "God give me vision and understanding to know what you want me to do and faith and strength and courage to do it." Now

I am going to tell a personal experience and I want you to note how my life was saved because I could understand what God was telling me and because I did it:

I was in Montana running a big ranch. We had had our first snow in November. It was light and drifted in patches. Had melted leaving patches of wet ground from 10 to 20 feet square. This had frozen hard. That morning we left the ranch house by daylight. In getting my horse I got my feet muddy. I had on a pair of boot-overshoes over my boots. When I put my feet in my stirrups they were hard to get out. We were gathering cattle out of a large pasture. The air was cold and crisp and my overshoes froze to the stirrups, making them like they were set in concrete and making them impossible to get out of the stirrups.

About 11 in the morning, these wet spots on the ground had thawed a little on top but froze hard except about a quarter of an inch on top. This made them exactly like plate glass covered with about one quarter inch of lard. I was riding a good cow pony and loped around a small bunch of steers to throw them in the herd. My horse stopped to turn on one of these wet spots and making a quick turn his feet went out from under him. The next thing I realized, I was under the horse with my feet froze in the stirrups; no chance to get them loose and my horse was up running and kicking me in the head. I did not see any way out. I simply looked up to God and said: "God, help me." Repeated it; then listened with all my mind. The thought came to me, which I consider God telling me, "Your bridle reins are still in your hand." I looked and realized they were. The next thought, "Pull your horse's head around to you and talk to him to quiet him." I did. The horse stopped still. The next thought, a cowboy was about a quarter of a mile from me but had not noticed anything wrong. "Call the cowboy." I did, and as the cowboy neared me, I told him to be careful and not scare my horse. He got down

from his horse; I told him to take my saddle off my
horse. He did and set me free.

Now you see there were several steps in this rescue.
I did not think I had a chance. I was not hurt at all. I
did not think up a way to escape. God directed me step
by step. I was not at any time scared. I was simply waiting and listening to God. Was it life or death? Whatever was God's will.

As you are a preacher and not a cowboy, you may not
be fully able to understand my situation, but I am sure
you know some good horsemen and if you will discuss it
with them I know that you will realize my position.

Now can we always get as clear directions as I did? I
would say "No." But we can always talk to God about
our troubles and trust God and try to find God's will
for us.

How mysteriously things happen to people who are simple
in their trust and who have faith and love in their hearts! During a visit to the Holy Land I met S. James Mattar, a Christian
Arab living in Jerusalem, Jordan. He was once an official of
Barclays Bank in the part of Jerusalem which is now in Israel.
Like many others, Mr. Mattar lost his job and home and his
possessions in the hostilities in that once embattled area.

He and his wife with their young children escaped across
the border to Bethany in Jordan. They arrived unharmed, but
practically penniless. Dark days followed; indeed the time
came when Mattar had exactly two shillings to his name and
no prospects of more money or any way of providing food for
his family.

But this man had an unquestioning faith in God. Gathering his wife and children around him, he humbly asked God's
blessings upon each of them and prayed for guidance. As he
prayed he got the distinct impression that he was to take some
empty baskets and go to the market place, accompanied by
Samuel, his eldest son.

On the way to the market Samuel said, "But, Papa, we have no money with which to buy anything." Mattar simply told him, "This is what the Lord has told me to do."

At the market they sat down and waited for what might happen. Presently a man came toward them through the crowd, greeting Mattar with the words, "How glad I am to see you, my old friend! I have had you very much on my mind of late and have been trying to locate you." He was a former employee of Barclays Bank and a friend from the old days.

The two men chatted but Mattar said nothing about the dire straits he was in. At length the other man, in a hesitant, embarrassed way, drew from his pocket a five pound note and said, "Would it be presumptuous to think that perhaps you are having difficulties? Please accept this for friendship's sake." Mattar was so overwhelmed that he could scarcely utter his thanks.

After the God-sent friend had departed Samuel asked, "Papa, did you know that man was going to pass by?"

"No, Sammy, I did not," Mattar replied. "We are in God's hands and He is good. You have just seen a demonstration of His providence."

The provisions purchased with the five pounds tided the Mattar family over until help reached them in the form of United Nations relief. Later on, Mr. Mattar found means of self-support. He is keeper of the Garden Tomb which is believed to be the tomb belonging to Joseph of Arimathea in which the body of Jesus lay. He is a spiritually inspiring friend. And his life and that of his wife is dedicated to helping other people in Christ's name.

Pondering Mr. Mattar's experience, I am impressed by the realization that if he had not had faith enough to act upon the guidance given in his prayer, he would not have received the help he desperately needed.

The result of prayer is not always so dramatic though no less real. A letter recently received from a reader describes how prayer in a time of deep trouble produced the direction and guidance that solved the problem.

"I felt," the letter reads, "as though I were in a dense, dark forest. In desperation I repeated the Lord's Prayer over and over, a dozen times a day. No spectacular events took place immediately. Little by little, however, I began to notice that always I could see one step ahead —and after I had taken that step, something would happen to enable me to see another step.

"A feeling came over me that some power was at work. I then began to think about God in earnest. I saw that in times of crisis something always happened that saved the day—not something planned by me, but some queer, unexpected circumstance. And I saw that the hard things in my life had worked for my good. . . ."

For the person who has the faith and courage to deal with difficulties a step at a time and leave tomorrow's problems and decisions in God's hands, circumstances often seem to develop in strangely beneficent ways. Faith does not necessarily get us everything we want. But it does make possible good results which otherwise might not happen. That it does shape events we can hardly doubt.

Mr. Mattar's experience demonstrates that some of the greatest answers to prayer come when you can do nothing at all for yourself and humbly realize that fact. Then you are really able to throw yourself trustingly upon God's help. "When I was hemmed in, thou has freed me often." (Psalm 4:1 Moffatt) This hemming in seems to create the type of situation in which God's providence is often remarkably demonstrated.

I am aware, of course, that some do not share my confidence in prayer to the extent described in this chapter. The reason could very well be that such dubious persons actually do not pray. One thing is certain, you will never get results from prayer if you never pray. How could you? And it may be that while perhaps you do pray, at least now and then, it is mostly in crisis or it is only perfunctory or formal.

It could be, of course, that your prayer effort is sincere and honest but still results fail to come. In that case the trouble could be caused by spiritual insulation—that is to say your personality may be insulated against God's power and goodness by resentment, evil thoughts and actions, negative thinking or other non-spiritual manifestations. In such case your prayers can't get through to God for the simple reason that they never get out of you. They cannot escape from the self-imposed insulation hence they never get off the ground, so-to-speak. Moreover, God's power which tends to flow toward you is blocked off not because you do not desire this power, for you do very much indeed; but it just cannot get into your personality because of the mental insulations you have created. When such thoughts and actions are removed power will flow in with a rush. Things will then be changed because you are changed.

Sum-up of *Pray Your Way Through Difficulty*

1. Break the tension by shifting your thoughts completely from the problem and instead think only about God. When you return to the problem your insight will sharpen; your understanding deepen.

2. Practice a daily quiet time in which to listen intently for God's direction; listen more deeply than your own thoughts.

3. Take God as your partner in every enterprise.

4. Apply analytical spiritual thinking about every problem.

5. Practice the write-it-out and put-it-in-the-Bible method and write your problems in the fewest possible words. Simplicity requires mental clarity and out of clarity clear answers come.

6. When you pray ask the Lord for directions as to what to do and how to do it. Then believe what He tells you. Do as He says.

7. Keep your mental and spiritual "contact points" cleaned so that God can operate through your mind.

TEN

HOW TO BE SUCCESSFUL AND HAPPY AND WHAT'S WRONG WITH THAT?

"Guess I'm mixed up or something. Do you suppose maybe I need straightening out?"

This semi-tongue-in-cheek question was asked by a twenty-four-year-old man, three years out of college, who had plunged enthusiastically into sales promotion. And he was doing well, too, exceptionally so.

"Mixed up?" I echoed. "Not you, from what I hear about you and your work performance you're anything but mixed up. I'm told you are a natural born salesman, that your record of production is going to hit the top if you keep going as you've begun. Don't try to make me think you're mixed up. You're not the mixed up kind."

"Well I just wonder whether maybe I'm wrong in wanting to be a creative and successful person, happy in my job and happy in myself." His attitude was half humorous and jovial but I could sense annoyance beneath his easy manner.

"I don't follow you," I replied. "What's worrying you anyway?"

"Here is what I mean. And I'm more concerned about the

effect on other young people than myself. You see I'm active in my church as well as in business. Guess I'm just made that way. Anything I go for I go all out for. I like to give it all I've got. I believe in maximum participation. I get a bigger charge out of it that way.

"I went to a couple of youth conferences in college and what I heard there got to me. They seemed to be real spiritual meetings and I decided to be a dedicated Christian, one who really means to live out his religion in every aspect of his life, personally, socially, in business, everything. This I have been doing and maybe that explains in part at least why I've been successful and happy too."

"But what has happened?" I inquired, realizing there was a resentment somewhere in this efficient young fellow's thinking.

"Well, you see we have a new pastor in our church. He is a scholar, you might even say an intellectual. Brother, you ought to hear his sermons. They sail right over the heads of most of the people like a balloon. I can hang on fairly well, for I'm only recently out of the collegiate atmosphere where you hear all those $64 words. He's a good guy at heart, I'm sure, but I just can't quite dig him. To hear him lay it out, you'd actually think that success is a dirty word; that you cannot be a Christian and a success at the same time. And he even takes a dim view of happiness; asks whether anyone has what he glumly calls 'the right to be happy in such a world as this.' Boy, is he on the sour side. As for businessmen he regards them as a bunch of crooks or Republicans or something. It's hard to figure which are worse."

"Well," I said, "judging from a recent *Reader's Digest* article on 'How 29 Companies Got Into Trouble' a lot of shady stuff does go on."

"Even so," he continued, "I must admit, I've got a grudging

admiration for this Reverend for he has a pretty good mind, if only he would live in this world. But his arguments, and that's what his sermons are, have hammered a halfway sense of guilt, or something, into me. If I want to please him I guess the only thing to do is to fail in business and be just plain unhappy. Maybe I'd better become a beatnik or a half-baked socialist. Apparently I'd do better sitting around bored like, living in a garage and growing long hair and blabbering a mess of existentialism or something. Nuts!" he concluded contemptuously.

"Listen," I said, "you have as much right to interpret Christianity as your pastor. He isn't the sole authority. Study it for yourself. Let him take a negative and bitter attitude if he wants to. It's a free country. You also have the right to draw strength, joy, courage, love, good will and creative satisfaction out of your faith; in other words, success and happiness."

Of course I know exactly how he reacted to his young pastor's ideas for this type of minister has criticized me for years, usually with hateful violence, for teaching people to think positively and make something creative of themselves. In fact they get so irritated over the subject of success that I have wondered whether many of these critics aren't just plain jealous of people who do something with their lives and their talents. A real Christian, the kind with the love of God and love of people in his heart rejoices when others gain victories and attain positive results over adversity and difficulty.

"But he riles me up," expostulated the young man.

"Oh, come on, don't let him do that to you. It isn't worth that expenditure of energy on your part. Anyway he is probably a better fellow than you think. Listen respectfully to him when he speaks in church, and then make him listen respectfully to you when you speak out of church. Our religion teaches us to think and let think, so let him think what he chooses. That's his right; and you think what you choose, that's your right. And then just go on doing a good job and be happy doing it.

"You have not only the right but the duty to be happy and successful and I don't care two cents worth who tells you that you haven't. And there is nothing at all inconsistent with Christianity in so doing. If this world was designed to produce unhappy, bored failures then it wasn't made by the creative God I believed in. I seem to remember that Jesus Christ himself said 'These things have I spoken unto you, that my joy remain in you, and that your joy might be full.' " (John 15:11)

I felt it my duty to be sure that this young man's concept of success checked with his faith, for obviously if it did violence to his religious principles, he could very well find himself in a real conflict. So I requested him to define success. "Is it to get a pile of money, belong to a snooty country club, run with a sophisticated crowd and swagger around in a sports car?" I asked.

"I am not quite so out of it as to hold that horse-and-buggy concept of success. The old money, power, big-shot success idea has gone by," he replied. "We're modern now and we've got a modern idea of success."

I rather liked that angle and voiced the opinion that some of the most pathetic failures I had ever known were wealthy people. They had money, but that is all. Or more accurately, the money had them. Beyond the ability to buy what they wanted they were complete flops as persons and as citizens. Perhaps, if these particular people had had practically no money they might have become very successful and happy persons.

Of course, I have also known some people who had very little and who were likewise failures; who had neither the manhood nor the character to do anything worthwhile with the little they did have. It's what you do with what you are, with what you have or don't have, that figures largely in determining failure or success.

Actually, these rich failures and poor failures have much in common. The rich failure never gives from his abundance, the poor failure never gives from his limitation. Neither contributes the best thing each has to give, namely himself. Neither the rich failure nor the poor failure cares except for himself, the one hugging his riches, the other his poverty. Neither cares anything about the world and its problems. In short, both are self-centered. All rich people are not bad and all poor people are not good. This is a fact the wise man learns as he matures. But, of course, some people never mature.

The "modern" idea of success held by our young friend intrigued me. "It is to be successful as a person," he said, "which means integrated and controlled within yourself, and integrated and controlled in your relationship with the group. To be successful is to be organized, quiet, assured, philosophical, urbane, confident and courageous. (All of that, no less.) It is to be outgoing, helpful, concerned, caring and constructive. (All adjectives which apply.) It is to give of yourself and of what you possess for social ends. In short, you might say it is to make everything and everyone you touch a little bit better. If you don't do these things, if you are not these things, you're no success, that's for sure."

"But how about becoming vice president of the company, or even president, getting a big salary and a cut of the take. Isn't that being successful and happy?" I asked.

"Sure, that's O.K. provided you are also successful as a person. And there is another point; if you make some dough your responsibility for its responsible use increases. The rich failure crudely thinks that money is simply to grease life's pathway for him, to add to his own comfort and security. But the rich success is a responsible person who administers his money with a sense of social obligation, even opportunity; and furthermore, he actually sees himself as a steward of wealth all of which really belongs to God. He is simply God's agent in handling money creatively. So where does the pastor get this pious stuff about nobody can make and have money and still be a Christian? He's a fuzzy thinker, if you ask me."

"You've got to get this minister out of your hair," I told my young friend. "If you let people rile you like this, you won't be successful as a person yourself. You are working yourself up into a first-class resentment of this theological sobersides. Better start thinking of him as a human being, one who is himself in trouble. He is sort of disorganized in his thinking, I'd say. No doubt he became a minister in the first place because of some real spiritual motivation. Then he enrolled in a seminary where he figured he would go deeper into spiritual understanding but they probably proceeded to drain off his religious impulses and gave a scolding twist to his thinking. In fact, they may have diverted him from religion as such to a piously oriented sociology. The result of that is often a mixing up and twisting of the minds of everyday people who would otherwise take an uncomplicated and usually true view of life and society.

"I seem to recall the philosopher Santayana saying something to the effect that the person who gives a wrong twist to your mind meddles with you as certainly as if he had hit you in the nose. So you had better start loving your pastor and try to untwist his mind. It could be that one function of laymen is to help modify the distortions resulting from some theological education; and I say some, for not all schools of theology siphon off religion. But as some cases have shown, it takes maybe from five to ten years of working among the plain people for some young pastors to recover the sense of perspective and balance which they may have lost in the seminary.

"But get this fact; this modifying process is not designed to force a pastor into thinking as you do or to make him accept your views. Maybe, just maybe, you as a business man don't know everything either. It is to bring him and you to the place where you can live in an attitude of mutual esteem, together finding workable answers to life's problems."

"I buy that," he said. "O.K. I will go on being as successful as God wants me to be and," he grinned, "I'll have the guts to be happy, too, without a sense of guilt along with it. And I'll work on that loving business too," he added quickly.

I was glad for his decision and his later attainment of both success and happiness for I have been encouraging my readers along these lines for years; and why not?

I have emphasized that one of the greatest aids to both success and happiness is a serious reading and study of the Bible which imbeds its truths deeply into consciousness. Some professors and preachers have roundly lambasted me for what they call, in their superior way, "using" religion.

But so what! Religion is designed to be used to help us live this life with some degree of success. And the more completely you identify religion with contemporary life the better world you will have, and better people, too. So let the critics rave and depreciate the effort to help people by relating God's word to daily problems. They leave me completely cold. I shall go right on doing my little bit in helping people to make their lives as complete and satisfying and as God-guided as is possible in this tough world.

It is shocking to realize that some ministers apparently haven't a faith that is big and vital enough to enable them to cope with the real world of men so not being able to handle its problems they make a getaway into the sheltered cloisters of religion to avoid being soiled by what they call "the un-ethical and unjust economic system."

William Cohea tells about three such men. "While speaking recently at Union Theological Seminary," he says, "my thesis concerning the ministry of the laity in the world was attacked. The attackers were three men who had just left the industrial world and had come to the seminary.

"The most irate of them all (why, may I interject, are they always irate? I wonder!) was a man who had been in industry eighteen years. He stated emphatically that while he had been in industry he had sought to minister to the needs of his fellows. In fact, 'My desk was a counselling center.' But after eighteen years he had decided that he loved the Lord so much that he had to go into the clergy.

" 'Why the clergy?' I asked.

" 'This is where one can *really* serve Christ,' he answered.

" 'But were you not serving Christ on your job as a layman?'

" 'Yes and no,' he continued. 'You see one cannot *really* be Christian in the industrial world. The conflict was too great for me. Compromise, compromise and conflict is all there is there. So, I decided that the only place where one can *really* serve Christ is in the ministry. So, here I am in seminary, and already I have a church.'

" 'Now tell me,' I asked. 'What do you tell the men who come to you from industry and are filled with compromise and conflict?'

" 'I understand them and can speak their language. One recently said it was wonderful to have a clergyman who knew their language.'

" 'Yes,' I said, 'and what do you tell them to do if they get fully dedicated to Christ? Do you tell them to leave industry and go into the ministry?' "

No answer. Of course not. These men were fooling themselves. They simply couldn't take the responsibility of living in the world so they lit out for a protected haven.

Well some of us who do have what it takes to live in the real world and still follow Christ and commit our lives to God believe that the Bible may be used as a practical instrument in achieving success as we have defined it and real happiness along with it.

As chairman of the Horatio Alger Committee of the American Schools and Colleges Association, I have been privileged for many years to present the Horatio Alger Award annually to a dozen top business or professional men chosen for this honor by vote of the students of America. These men are living demonstrations of the opportunity of a free enterprise economy, men who from lowly beginnings have created vast enterprises and helped build our country's life to higher standards for all our people. These men are true tough-minded optimists.

One of this group is Alfred C. Fuller, once an awkward country boy from Nova Scotia who built the immense Fuller Brush Company which grosses more than one hundred million dollars annually. Mr. Fuller, a lovable personality called "Dad Fuller" by his associates, is charmingly depicted by Hartzell Spence in *A Foot in the Door,* a fascinating book.

Fuller who claims to have been an awkward blundering boy when he came to Boston to get work says this awkwardness lost him several jobs, indeed it clung to him for quite some time. But as is well known ultimately he became a very wise and competent industrialist. How? Through the study of the Bible he says. In fact he established his plant in Hartford, Connecticut for no other reason than that the Fuller's old family Bible back home in Nova Scotia had been printed in that city.

Here is what Mr. Fuller has to say about the use of the Bible in his business experience:

> What most impresses me, as I look backward, is the immense application I have made of Bible truths in my daily life. My deficient formal schooling was, in the

sum of my life, no liability, but perhaps an asset. From
lack of education, I relied on the Bible as my textbook
in every conceivable problem that arose. Only when I
deviated from this teaching, or attempted to interpret the
message erroneously to accommodate my own desires,
did I fail.

He who does not live daily in its guidance is foolish
for he is rejecting the greatest source of personal profit
that exists in the world. The Bible is the best how-to-
do-it book ever compiled, and it covers every fundamental that anyone really needs to know.

Fuller had total lack of knowledge of cost accounting, pric-
ing, even bookkeeping and according to his own appraisal he
was deficient in management techniques including the handling of people. He humbly realized that he lacked these
qualities which are so essential to success. Experience with
his most vital employees made him realize that the time had
come to evolve a definite philosophy as an employer. He tells
about his method as follows:

As usual in moments when I needed infallible advice
on matters beyond my comprehension, I studied my
Bible for enlightenment. Finally I came on this passage
in Luke: "When thou art bidden of any man to a marriage feast, sit not down in the chief seat, lest haply a
more honorable man than thou be bidden. And he that
bade thee shall come and say to thee, Give this man
place; and then thou shalt with shame take the lower
place. But when thou art bidden, go and sit down in
the lowest place, that when he that hath bidden thee
cometh, he may say to thee, Friend, go up higher."
(Luke 14:8-10)

All three of my workers deserved higher places than I
in their own skills. I saw that building a business was
essentially a matter of manpower possessed of facilities

which I lacked. How then to reward them and what should my attitude be toward them? The Book of Matthew gave me a suggestion: "He that was sown upon the ground, this is he that heareth the word, and understandeth it; who verily beareth fruit, and bringeth forth, some a hundredfold, some sixty, some thirty." (Matthew 13:23)

From these passages I concluded that personal elevation at the expense of my associates was unsound. I must remain as I was, and find from among those about me the stock that would bear good fruit, and reward each man according to his contribution. Just because I owned the business, I was no better than anyone else. We were all in this together, and would rise or fall with it. If I remembered this, I knew that I also would grow in stature and in the ability to contribute.

In handling life and its problems successfully it is important to acquire a basic know-how and by basic I mean a deeper connotation even than technical information. This know-how in depth may be described by an old and rather disused word: *wisdom*. When you possess wisdom and a subtle understanding of life and its primary principles you can develop into a thoroughly knowledgeable person, one who has know-how, sagacity, insights and skills. And the wise person has another quality which Americans used to set great store by, called in the old vernacular *common sense*. This quality actually made the American economy, representing as it did the ability to take basic human needs and apply to them study and inquiry and come up with constantly improved methods and processes. Yankee common sense stimulated the spectacular successes this country produced and contributed largely to the happiness and well-being of vast numbers of people. It goes without saying that it also created stresses, injustices, inequities and problems galore. But it must be remembered that inherent in the system are not only its weaknesses but also its own correction and renewing power as well.

This common sense which is so important to success and happiness carries with it a concomitant characteristic, mention of which no doubt falls unpleasantly upon some modern ears.

In fact some of our smart lads write it off as "corny"—their quaint term for man-sized attitudes foreign to them. I refer to that down-to-earth quality which stimulates and maintains drive. In plain English I mean just hard work, the guts to keep at it, letting nothing stand in the way of attaining a goal or objective, and to get a lot of fun out of the process.

True this drive-motivation has produced a few nervous wrecks, and neurotics, but it has also developed innumerable happy and successful persons which is why we are for it. I know for a fact that hard work makes you happy because I have worked hard all my life and I'm happy. I went to work as a boy for the simple reason that I had to as I wanted to eat and I had no small appetite. There have been a few times, I must admit, when I got fed up with the program of constant work and then more work. So I tried to loaf but I could never take it for very long. I just wasn't happy loafing. There must be a screw loose in a man who turns out to be a playboy. While there may be some people who actually like the innocuous kind of living in which they indulge, I have never personally met one whom you could honestly call a really happy person. They frustrate their God-given sense of creativity, and you have to develop that to be either happy or successful.

Of course, there are plenty of people who will tell you that hard work doesn't get you anywhere nowadays as it did in the old times. I've heard that melancholy tune played by weaklings so often that I almost fell for it myself but not quite, I'm thankful to say. Now I don't believe it at all.

And one reason for my conviction is John M_____. And
who is John M_____? Well in my book he is one of the
finest and realest Americans I have ever known.

It was in Sorrento, Italy that I first met John. My wife and
I like that charming coastline up past Ravello and Amalfi to
Sorrento dreaming above the Bay of Naples. But there was
one citizen of that town who was doing more than dreaming
though he had his share of dreams tucked up under the heart
too.

On the square in Sorrento is a shop that my wife went for
completely. I got the notion she was buying out the place.
"You," I said, "are a babe in the woods to these alert sales-
clerks. They can sell you anything." Personally, I wouldn't
even go into the shop. "I don't want anything they've got.
Besides I'm an old hand at traveling and they couldn't sell me
a plugged nickel."

"Yes, dear, I know. They wouldn't try to sell you for they
could see at once that you are too smart for them. Just come
on in and get out of this hot sun anyway." Sweetly she be-
guiled me and led me to the linen department where soon I
was signing traveller's checks for her purchases.

Then up strolled a pleasant Italian boy who offered me a
refreshing Coca Cola. He seemed quite interested in America and in me personally and we had a delightful talk. Soon
I found myself in the furniture department listening to a
charming description of how the beautiful pieces were made.
It was all so disarming and pleasant and an hour later I was
excitedly buying an entire set to be shipped home.

"Boy, you are some salesman," I said admiringly to John
M_____. "As they say back home—you could sell the Brooklyn Bridge. You would really go places in the U.S.A."

"That's where I want to go," he said. "I have an American
wife and we both want to go to the United States to live. I've

never been there. My wife came here to visit. She stayed when she met me."

"You sold her, too, eh?" I grinned. "What's stopping you from coming to America?" I asked.

He mentioned some of the difficulties involved. "Just make up your mind you're coming and when you do," I went all out in my enthusiasm, "when you do, let me know and I'll get you a job." Then I outlined to him the techniques of Positive Thinking and told him I would have a copy of my book *The Power of Positive Thinking* sent to him airmail.

Did he read the book? That's not the half of it. About a month before Christmas, my secretary said, "A young man wants to see you. Says he's a friend of yours from Italy."

"A friend from Italy . . . ? What's he want?"

"He says he wants that job you promised him."

"I didn't promise anyone a job." I live a busy life and the incident in Sorrento had slipped my mind. "What is the name of this fellow?"

"John M_____," she replied. Sure enough here was John, big as life.

"How did you get here?" I asked.

"Through God's help and positive thinking, how do you think?" was his conclusive answer.

So it was up to me to deliver on my promise to find a job for John. I wrote letters to the heads of a half dozen of the leading stores in New York, each letter showing that copies had been sent to other fine stores. Some of these men I knew personally, some I didn't; but I said something like this: "In Sorrento, Italy I met one of the greatest natural-born salesmen I've ever known. He is here in New York, ready to go to work for the employer lucky enough to get him. The first one to ask for him, gets him." Before the week was over he was hired by an important men's clothing shop.

"I'm going to work hard and give it all I've got," said John.

"I am going to get ahead and be a real part of this wonderful country." His eyes were shining with love for America, land of boundless opportunity. That utterly fascinating thing called the American dream was burning in him. Though he could not define it, it was the Horatio Alger tradition: up from the bottom, the sky is the limit, nothing too good to be true for the man who will work for it.

I hesitated. Should I enlighten him on the cynical notion that nowadays it's "corny" to dream like that, that only "dopes" work hard, that a man isn't "playing ball" with the other employees who tries to do a really good job? Should I tell him how some labor bosses penalize the man who wants to work hard and do better work? Should I tell him about those "respectable" thieves who steal the boss's time, as well as his merchandise? Should I tell him about the phonies who run businesses, who are perfectly willing to let a fellow burn himself out and then deny him the advancement that he has earned?

No, not I. It isn't my job to disillusion men but rather to encourage them in their highest ideals and I believe in ideals, for ideals are tough and good. When a man's ideals are the real thing even such revoltingly dishonest and sordid happenings cannot puncture them. Such a man may get wise to what goes on but still he lives above it. And, thank God, it is still possible to live above this shoddy stuff in America. And the man who does live above and who stays above goes on up. He goes places, top places and he stays there. And that is exactly what John did.

The Christmas business ended, extra clerks were let go—all but John. The manager said, "The only job I have is selling hats. We have a vacancy in that department but hat selling isn't too hot right now. It's the style to go bareheaded and be collegiate."

"Well," said John, "I've never worn a hat but a hat salesman is exactly what I want to be. When do I start?"

The first sale John made was to himself. If he was going to sell hats he had to know hats. He got so sold on wearing hats that it wasn't long until he was selling nearly every man who came along. And he figured out ways to get them coming along and to keep them coming.

Naturally, a boy like John was noticed. He was different and different people cannot help but be noticed. And what was different about him? He worked. He didn't loaf and he was happy. He radiated something. He was enthusiastic. He believed in hats. He loved to sell hats. He definitely tried to sell hats, not one hat, but two or three for different outfits like the women do. He wasn't like the clerk in the hardware store who was approached by a customer who asked for a paint brush. What do you think the clerk did. He sold the man the paint brush, but just the brush he asked for. But did he try to sell him an extra one, and some paint to go with the brush and some turpentine? The customer got just what he asked for, didn't he?

This same customer told me that the same sad process was repeated in three stores. These clerks of course were not salesmen. They were only order takers. No wonder such men never got anywhere, and no doubt, they have much to say about there being no opportunity in the United States anymore; and they probably vote for left wingish candidates at election time who sneer at the free enterprise system, glib men who, like themselves, blame the system and not their own difficulties.

I heard of a man who made a test in several men's furnishing stores. He came in and said to a clerk, "My luggage went astray in an airlines baggage mix-up. I haven't a thing except what's on me. I'd like to buy a shirt." Did the clerk also try to sell him socks, ties, pajamas, underwear, the common necessities? What do you think? Believe it or not, none did until he came to store number five, where the experiment was again repeated. There the test customer encountered a real salesman: a clerk who was alert and more than a robot order-taker. He sold the customer a full outfit and a suitcase to carry it away.

So John was noticed by the hat manufacturer. Result, he is today a national sales manager of a big hat manufacturing organization.

Who said America isn't still the land of opportunity? It certainly is for the man who has within him the capacity for opportunity and every man has that if he only knows it. John is a happy successful man. He is a godly man, a sincere Roman Catholic, a good father, a great American and my dear friend. He is a real tough-minded optimist. He inspires me to be a better salesman myself. And in a sense I am a salesman too, trying to communicate and gain acceptance for ideas, ideas that can change a man's life. I'm a salesman for the greatest of all ideas—faith, a faith that can lift a man into a wholly new and wonderful world of experience. And frankly I hope you'll buy it.

I know that some who read this book would like to acquire and possess the spirit and attitudes we are describing but they have perhaps lost faith in themselves. The old enthusiasm has hit bottom. Then what? Just get busy getting it back again, that's the answer. And how is that done? Well, who made you alive in the first place? God, of course, and He can make you come alive again. So, if you are dull, desultory, dopey, or just plain disillusioned, the first step in your revitalization is to re-emphasize God in your life. It's just that simple.

"Well," you may ask, "but just how is that done? It sounds pretty complicated and vague to me."

Let me give you one technique which I have used on myself, for don't think I haven't also had the problem of losing faith in myself, and the declining enthusiasm that goes along with it. This hits everyone at some time or other.

My method is to get off by myself and sit quietly until I achieve a fairly relaxed state of mind and body. Then I practice conceiving of God, the Creator, as actually touching me, actually re-creating me, then and there. I consciously "feel" new life passing from Him into my body, into my mind. I picture my spirit as being renewed again, then and there—not later but right then. I see myself as making vital electric contact. I then say aloud slowly the following statement, "In Him (I) live, and move, and have (my) being." (Acts 17:28) The three dynamic elements in that scripture text are: *identification* (I live in Him), *energy* (I move), *completion* (have my being). As a result of this procedure I feel an actual renewal, sensory, mental and spiritual. It really works.

I then remind myself that within me are all the qualities, abilities, thoughts and impulses necessary to successful and satisfying life. I say aloud the following dynamic words, and they are dynamic too, for they produce and transmit power: ". . . the kingdom of God is within you." (Luke 17:21) To personalize it I use the pronoun *me*. I shall never forget the first time the full meaning of those words dawned on me. The way I figured it was that a king was always rich and powerful. He had everything to make life good. God is the greatest King of all; He has everything in His hands. So therefore all of the riches of God's kingdom; His power, peace, joy, health are in essence built into me as His child, whom He Himself created. He put it all into me, and into you, for our use.

All at once as in a flash, I saw myself as possessing "riches" in the form of strength, courage, peace, capacity, whereas I had thought I was completely out of these assets. I then knew that I had only to draw upon them as gifts of God, which He had placed in me because He knew I would need them in living a full and complete life. And when you really draw upon them and live upon them with confidence and joy you have them in abundant supply and you can keep on drawing and the supply is never exhausted.

Try it and see for yourself. Successful and happy living was built into you by God who created you.

If you have never experienced this kind of life, maybe you need to be re-created. And it takes God to do that for you. But He will do it. Then you will receive the insight and spiritual know-how to overcome one of our most defeating factors, the self-destruction tendency.

An old friend, Fred H_____, discovered this to be true. He had a tough time with himself and with life, but he found his answer. Fred's trouble was that he had unwittingly encouraged his own self-destructiveness. And, as I say, tragically we all have within us the capacity for self-destructiveness. Good and bad are in us, heaven and hell, the Kingdom of God and the Kingdom of the devil. Which gets on top and stays there is the issue, or as Shakespeare says in ten significant words: "To be, or not to be: that is the question."

We all face the psychological and spiritual problem of the opposites; weakness or strength, fear or faith, positive thinking or negative thinking. So while the destruction tendency is in us, so also is the creative impulse. The technique for overcoming self-destructiveness is to stress the opposite or the creative factor which is within us.

It is important to realize that men are not primarily destroyed by other people, or by conditions or by situations, or even by society or government. Basically they are destroyed by their own complex and frustrating tendency to self-destructiveness. And they can be saved from this by the creative tendency which God has put into every human being.

Fred H_____ found it so and I watched him struggle with it across the years, helping as I could. But Fred found his own renewing answer and, in the last analysis, it is only your own answer that really answers your problems. But let Fred H_____ tell his own story, which he does in the following letter:

> Dear Norman:
>
> Thirty-two years ago this March, you married S_____ and me. For the next eighteen years I lived a comparatively average sensible life. My above average position in a utilities company provided a comfortable living for my family.
>
> Then in 1946, I became unaccountably dissatisfied and created my own reasons for leaving my job. I became a professional entertainer at the worst time in show business history. Two years in this precarious field with many long trips away from home brought me to my senses and also a world of despair. I began to lean on liquor to drown my self-disgust.
>
> In an effort to right myself I tried to arrange for reinstatement with the utilities company. You and others wrote letters in my behalf. The effort failed. I was then 44 and found it difficult to find gainful employment. I became a house-to-house salesman and spasmodically earned a fair living. I was, however, constantly full of self-hatred and ashamed of the self-imposed act that had brought my wife and adopted sons to a very low state of insecurity.
>
> Whenever I applied for a full time position in an established company no one could believe that a responsible man of past 40 would leave the utilities company to do what I had done! I was at that time completely dejected and beaten.
>
> My wife had taken a job as a night nurse and in addition to her duties tried to run our home and care for our sons. My income had shrunk lower and lower. I had however stopped drinking and had resolved that no matter what happened I would face life soberly.
>
> Every morning when my wife arrived home and be-

fore I would start out on calls, we would take 15 minutes to pray, to read the Bible and to ask God to direct us. We would write down our thoughts and the ideas that came. I still have those notes and I can tell you that they are my most prized possessions.

On one of these mornings it was necessary for me to take our old car to a garage for a major repair job. Instead of going to the man who had repaired our car for many years, it seemed very clear to me that I should go to another shop in a different part of the city. I knew the proprietor but had not seen him in 20 years. I did just that! When I returned for my car at the end of the day a smart looking foreign car was parked along side of mine. As I was admiring it the car's owner arrived. We introduced ourselves, said a few pleasantries and he drove off. I learned from the garage man that he owned a radio station, that he had had severe financial trouble but had fought his way back to the top.

Several days passed and I thought nothing more of the garage incident. Then one morning when S_____ and I were praying, the man's face and the whole experience flashed through my mind. I decided then and there to find him, tell him my story and offer my services. I did. As I reached the radio station he was waiting for a car to take him to the airport. I suggested that I drive him there. We did. He said there were no openings. I said (and I remember every word) "I want desperately to get into this business. My background in various fields lends itself to your type of enterprise and I will be an asset to you." He looked intently at me and said, "Come to the station as often as you like, stay there as many hours as you wish, get my boys to show you the ropes, learn the controls, learn how to read news. At the end of two weeks, if you are any good, I'll put you on the payroll at $50 a week and pay you a commission of sales." I accepted. That was in January 1956. Within a month I was number-two newsman and at the end of the second month I was offered the manager's position. In March of this year I will begin my fourth year here as manager and I have just been named president of our corporation. Norman, every day I thank God many times for leading me here. In three short, glorious years I have been able to recoup my losses and now earn a handsome salary and receive a percentage of certain profits.

From a morose, despondent person who had daily contemplated suicide, I am now very active and alert. I have been accepted in Rotary, my work made it possible to become a member of a journalistic fraternity.

We play golf at the local country club and S_____ and I at age 56 have joined the Figure Skating Club and have learned how to skate. We do that three times a week and are having more fun than the kids. Also I try to keep ahead of my son in algebra and after 25 years have taken up the five-string banjo again for relaxation.

If this account will help anyone, you are at liberty to use it in any way you wish. But please camouflage names and places—I don't want any more glory than my experience has already given me. It has shown me that miracles still happen. I am one by the Grace of God.

Fred H_____ overcame his tendency to self-destruction through God's guidance and spiritual re-creation. He learned to draw upon the Kingdom of God which was within him all the time. He is now a happy and successful man.

Every morning as you start the day say those powerful words: The Kingdom of God is in me—with God's help I can handle whatever comes. And when you know for a fact that you can do just that, and if you always keep humble, and work and pray—and are always a tough-minded optimist—you will live a happy and successful life and what's wrong with that?

Sum-up of *How To Be Successful and Happy*

1. Have absolutely no sense of guilt about being happy and successful if you operate honestly and with a sense of social responsibility.

2. Get the modern idea of success which is to be successful as a person.

3. Read and study the Bible as a practical guide to successful living.

4. Don't write off the importance of hard work, the guts to keep at it, a definite goal and the ability to have fun in the process. If there's no fun in it, something's wrong with all you're doing.

5. Use your head. Without that you'll never get ahead.

6. Keep enthusiastic and love what you're doing.

7. Keep relaxed. Don't tense up no matter what, for you only close off creative power when you do. The relaxed man is the powerful man.

8. Have quiet times regularly and practice the "feel" of God, your Creator, re-creating you.

9. Visualize the Kingdom of God as in you. See yourself as the potential possessor of God's bounty.

10. Eliminate—and this is very important—eliminate your capacity for self-destructiveness.

THE TOUGH-MINDED OPTIMIST
LOOKS AT THE CHURCH

At a luncheon a few of us were passing the time of day. Ever on the lookout for men to recruit for the spiritual life and it being just before Easter I said rather jovially, "Well, I suppose all you fellows will be in church on Sunday." One said he went every Sunday; two others, most of the time. The rest were more or less Easter-church-goers.

Then came a rather shocking and as it later proved, pathetic reaction. May I warn you that this will disturb you as it did me. I hope it isn't representative. I'm sure it's extreme but will give it to you unvarnished just as I experienced it.

One man showed anger and it was real anger, too. His eyes blazed and his face reddened as he growled, "Hell, no, I'll not be there and for that matter, never again. You can count me out of the church for good!"

Startled we all fumbled for words; an embarrassing silence fell. After a moment I ventured: "Please, what's on your chest?"

"These guys wouldn't be interested but I'll talk to you personally," he replied. That ended the conversation which left us all with an unpleasant feeling.

So, of course, I saw him later and he let me have it straight. He minced no words. It was pretty tough talk, believe me. "The church and all ministers can go straight to hell," he said. "And why not, for that's just where you're letting the rest of us go." He was very bitter.

I showed no reaction to his startling remark and let him go on. And scarcely in all my experience have I heard such resentment expressed toward churches and ministers in general. And the story was this:

This man had worked hard and, as he expressed it, "used my head in business and got ahead and made a big pile of dough." Then he and his wife decided to move to suburbia. "I had the money so we got everything: three cars, country club membership—the works. Before this I had been too busy to go in much for social life but now, having gotten up in the company, I had to make some special big deal contacts . . . big deal!" he spat out contemptuously. "They all make me sick. I could vomit when I think of those jerks. I'd rather have nothing and live on the fourth floor of a Third Avenue walk-up, as we once did, and have some peace of mind and happiness."

"Go on," I urged, "give me the facts without the philosophy. Why this gripe about churches and ministers?"

"O.K." he growled. "You asked for it, so I'll let you have it straight. It's because they let me go straight to hell and never once tried to stop me.

"You see it's this way. The neighbors began inviting us to cocktail parties. These were sedate affairs—and the people seemed nice. In fact, some of them are. Then we got into the party crowd and I realized we were drinking a lot. One night I found my wife with her arm draped over a guy's neck and she was soused to the gills. I dragged her home and put her to bed.

"I was pretty well pickled myself but was sober enough to

do some thinking . . . What else had she been doing with guys? Suspicion grew in my mind and I knew I wasn't too hot myself when it came to morality. However, I wasn't going to have a second-hand wife.

"Came morning and at breakfast Mary suddenly said, 'Jack, honey, what is the matter with us? I'm not enjoying all this suburbia stuff. It's no fun. Let's get out of this place before it's too late.'

" 'I feel the same way, Mary,' I replied and then, like a stupid dope, added: 'But we've got too big an investment here and I've got to stay in with the big shots. But I tell you what. Let's get back into going to church and meeting some nice church people. That will keep us on an evener keel and the preacher will help us stick to our moral standards.'

"So we started going around to a few churches to see which one we might like. But I didn't like any. The preachers sounded like a bunch of pedantic professors and every damned one of them sounded like lousy socialists. They couldn't fool me for I can smell a parlor pink a mile off. And not once did I hear a single word about sin, and sin was what I wanted to hear about because I was, and still am, full of it right up to my eyes. And that isn't all of it. The nice church people started inviting us and, Doctor Peale, believe it or not, their parties were not too much different from those of the non-churchgoers!"

He looked at me with pain in his eyes—call it agony, if you will. "Norman," he said, "I'm in hell. Mary and I have broken up. I just couldn't stomach a wife-trading party. It makes me want to throw up every time I think of it. She was too good for that, but she has gone all the way to hell now and so have I. Norman, for God's sake, why didn't the church help us before we hit the rocks like this?" He almost sobbed. "The church failed us. They let us down. They made us think that sin doesn't matter any more. The hell with 'em."

I sat in sadness. He was unreasonable, of course. He was full of self-pity and was floundering badly in his thinking, blaming everyone but himself for the crackup of his life. That he was wounded deeply was evident; and as a spiritual physician it was my duty to cleanse his wounds, reshape his thinking, help him find God's forgiveness, teach him to forgive himself, and help him rebuild his life on a sound spiritual and moral basis. He must be shown that the type of life that is really happy is the Christian life. And it is too for didn't Jesus say: "I am come that they might have life, and that they might have it more abundantly." (John 10:10)

Actually, this so-called sophisticated generation isn't so sophisticated at all. Sophistication means to know your way around in the world, to be worldly-wise. The denizens of suburbia, or "disturbia" as some now call it, in all too many cases really don't know their way around, for lots of them have been hurt like Jack and Mary—and they couldn't be very worldly-wise to mess up their lives in such unsmart ways. Real God-filled Christ-centered Christianity, with a mansize depth emphasis on sin and a faith that is full of the tremendous joy of spiritual experience could give these mixed-up citizens of suburbia a zest-packed life the like of which they never knew existed.

The old heavy, fear-ridden emphasis upon sin, the narrow-mindedness of some religious people in days gone by, may have in part stimulated the rebellion against morality which has now hit bottom in frustration, crime, nervous breakdown, broken marriages and personality collapse. But there is an answer and it is in those churches which teach a sound moral system, a life-changing Gospel and a Christian social program. The churches which know how to communicate this teaching to the modern mind in a convincing manner will be, in this generation as in the past, the salvation of men and society.

Thank God we have many churches of this type in suburbia, even though Jack didn't find one.

One night when I was bewailing the decline in man-sized, honest-to-goodness redemptive religion, my eighteen-year-old daughter Elizabeth, a college student, who often visits friends in a nearby suburban community, said, "Daddy, you don't know the whole story. I can tell you that the preacher in the church where I go when I visit my friends out there doesn't play games with them. He gives it to them straight and they take it, too." And what she said was true. Not only do they take it; they love him for it. Furthermore they respect him, and this minister, as well as others, has built a real church of dedicated people in the heart of suburbia—which shows that it can be done.

So the church isn't nearly as deficient or faulty, nor the ministers either, as Jack in his desperation made out. Ministers are of course human and sometimes they have been awed by the materialistic, pagan culture in which they work. A friend of mine, a sincerely spiritual, younger man moved into a swank mid-west suburban town and was invited to join a church informally called the executives' church. "But," he replied to the obviously socially polished pastor, "I have listened to several of your sermons but cannot figure out what you believe in. You are one of the most finished speakers I have heard but where do you stand on personal commitment to Christ and on Christ's Gospel for the world?"

The pastor explained, "The executive-type of people in this church will only take so much Christianity. You have to slip it to them easy or they will leave you. The golf course is tough competition."

"I don't go along with that," said my friend. "Beneath all this stuffed-shirt stuff, these are real people, and if you give them the real thing, most of them will go for it."

This man started a group in his own home for the discussion of Christ's answer to personal and social life, and to consider the meaning of personal commitment. So many people wanted to come that the original group has broken into a number of groups. The pastor himself joined and experienced a new birth of spiritual life. He is no longer afraid of the so-called big shots and these men really listen to him now. And why not? People will always listen to the man who has something to say and the courage to say it and the guidance to say it right.

If the church does not come through with a vital Gospel for the individual and society, men will find their answers outside the church, as did Ed M_____, head of a large business in a southern city. He came to see me with his fiancée to talk about their forthcoming marriage. I, of course, talked with them as any pastor does about building their married life on a spiritual foundation.

In the course of the conversation I asked if they were church-going people. The lady said she goes every Sunday, but he rather startled me by saying, "No, I never go to church. I'm an Episcopalian, but the Rector has absolutely nothing on the ball, so I just can't be bothered going."

"But," I said, "you puzzle me because I always thought of you as an enlightened man spiritually. I know your thinking and have been impressed by your victorious spirit."

"I can explain that," he said. "Every morning for one hour from 6:30 to 7:30 I read the Bible and spiritual books. Then I have my quiet time during which I write out my problems and surrender them to God asking for guidance. And I've been amazed by the guidance I've received. I wouldn't think of not living with Christ. It's the only answer to life." His face positively glowed as he said this.

Granted that he may be a pretty positive type of man, still I could not help feeling sorry for the Rector, no doubt a fine and true man, who couldn't communicate the Gospel and

have spiritual fellowship with a real fellow like Ed M_____,
especially since Ed M_____ wanted God with all his heart.

Nowadays people like Ed M_____ are finding increasingly a dynamic personal faith and they want to express it in
social action. But many are bewildered by what they call a
"leftist fringe which has wormed its way into some churches."
I hasten to add that, while I am constantly hearing this sort of
complaint, actually I'm quite certain it isn't as true as it may
appear.

For many years, like most ministers, I have been persuading
men to commit their lives to Christ and have found them responsive. I always try to relate men to the church as active
participants in its worship and in its social and world mission.

I believe I have encouraged a large number of men to become vital members. But it is not easy to hold some of them:
indeed, many have become very restive because of what they
heatedly describe as "leftist master-minding within church
bodies and the duping of otherwise good people into becoming
fellow-travelers." I cannot accept this point of view and have
persuaded not a few men to think differently and to hold
steady as church members. But since I can reach only a limited
number with personal conversation and have no access to
religious periodicals I want to use a brief portion of this book
to urge my readers to support the church as the spiritual
instrument for bringing in that form of substantial social
change called the Kingdom of God on earth. You may find
this chapter somewhat different from our usual emphasis but
it concerns a matter which I feel should be discussed and considered by thoughtful people.

Jeff H_____ was one man with whom I had quite a
difficult time for he was a tough-minded thinker, the kind
who asks searching questions and who is very smart, too. I
reached him originally through my National Council of
Churches radio program *The Art of Living*. He was on his

way to a golf course one Sunday morning and as he drove was listening to the car radio. My program came on. He said afterward that he listened because he had heard me speak at a national business convention and "kinda liked me."

In this radio talk, as in all of them, I tried to preach what you might call a luring kind of message, one definitely designed to attract, convince and persuade, the objective being to gain acceptance and commitment. Inasmuch as this man played golf every Sunday morning he formed the habit of listening to our program regularly on his way to the Country Club. The message, approached in various ways, hammered always on one idea: Your life can mean so much more. You need not be defeated by anything. Joy and peace can be yours and health and vitality and enthusiasm, too. Jesus Christ is the answer; indeed, He is your answer. Why not commit your life to Him? Then find a church. Become a vital part of its worship and work. Through it share your spiritual experience with other people. Be no longer a part of the world's problem but part of its cure and your life will be full of happiness and satisfaction and so, too, will the lives of others.

Jeff H_____ tells me that one morning he found himself thinking, I should do that. I should commit my life to Christ. But he never did anything hurriedly, without much thought and questioning. However, the idea had lodged in his mind and started working. The following Sunday he surprised his wife by saying, "Guess I'll go to church with you today and see what they're handing out over there."

As he told me this story at this point I held my breath. What kind of preacher would he find at that church? I hoped he wouldn't find a dry-as-dust super-duper intellectual, or pulpit-scold, or carping social-manifesto zealot, or one of those mechanical have-all-the-answers fundamentalists, especially one of those mean ones. I hoped he would find a sincerely dedicated, Christ-centered preacher, who had a message with some spiritual vitality in it. Hoping against hope I asked, "How was church?"

"It was great. The minister was a real guy. That was evident from the minute he started talking. He talked my language and he must have known I was there too, for he spoke to me directly. There was a lot of the good old Bible and sin in his sermon. He had none of that preachy stuff and none of that socialistic junk the fellows say preachers hand out nowadays. He told what being a Christian means in a way I could understand and it got to me.

I liked it so much that I shifted my time for golf and got to going to church pretty regularly. I didn't change my ways all at once, but they got me into a group of men where they study the Bible and discuss how to relate it to our lives and daily problems. Later on I got active in the church and I'm trying to grow spiritually like you said."

Then Jeff H_____ came to his present problem. "But, Norman, I'm bewildered." He pulled from his pocket several clippings. "Read that tripe," he barked, "just read that tripe." He sat back and sort of glared while I glanced at the clippings. I recognized them at once as various "pronouncements" issued by denominational and inter-denominational church meetings. And there were several full page "statements" signed by a number of ministers. Then he slapped a final clipping on my desk, an article with a big headline "PROTESTANTS URGE RECOGNITION OF RED CHINA. Cleveland Meeting Unanimous For Admission to U.N."

"Where do they get that stuff? I'm a Protestant and I'm not for that."

"Look, Jeff," I said, "why not look at it this way. Just realize that there is a style among a certain type of minister which may be classified as a speak-out, sign-statements, issue-pronouncements style. They call it "prophetic" or some such impressive term. This style has been developed over a period of years into a standardized attitude and any deviation from it they regard as a kind of treason. Indeed, they look superciliously down on you if you don't supinely go along. But personally I never did go along, unless I wanted to, whether they looked down or not. I insist upon the integrity of being myself and of determining my own pattern of thought."

"But what are they trying to prove with this stuff?" he asked. "Don't they have any interest at all in the spiritual life? There isn't a single solitary "pronouncement" about immorality, drunkenness, divorce, youth delinquency, homosexuality or dishonesty . . . nary a word! Guess they are not interested in anything except politics and in that department they smell like souped-up socialists . . . or communists, but I guess that would be too strong a word. What about this National Council of Churches? I'm suspicious of that outfit, too."

"Well, Jeff, you're throwing me a lot of questions all at one time and I'll try to answer them. But first I must caution you against taking a negative attitude toward people, no matter how you may feel toward them. That isn't in itself a spiritual approach, really. And don't get so 'het up' about it. Just go on developing your life in Christ and make your own Christian contribution to the problems of our time.

"And now, Jeff, let me answer your questions about the controversial National Council of Churches. I've been associated with their Broadcasting and Film Commission for years. Mrs. Peale has served as a vice president of the Council; and currently is, and has been for a number of years, a member of its General Board and of its highest-level committee, on policy and strategy. I may say that Mrs. Peale and I respect each other's thinking so much that we can, and frequently do, disagree; and my opinions are my own and hers are distinctly her own, and I mean *distinctly*.

"I have had some knowledge of this inter-denominational

church body for many years so feel that I know whereof I speak.

"Now, Jeff, as far as my knowledge goes, there is no reason to suspect Communistic infiltration of the National Council of Churches. Perhaps there are a few, a very few whose Communistic or fellow-traveler leanings may be suspicious; but they have never been in executive responsibility and actually never seemed to carry too much weight. The secretariat of the Council under Dr. Roy G. Ross and its body of delegates are, as far as I know, sincere Christian people who conscientiously attempt to give constructive spiritual leadership in contemporary society."

Jeff had listened attentively. "O.K. I'll accept your thinking and will try to understand these Christian leaders, but in my opinion some of them are pretty balmy," he said stubbornly.

The chief cause of widespread misunderstanding concerning the Council is due I believe to a small nest of what you might call starry-eyed do-gooders who in their social-political crusading zeal are actually weakening the influence of this great church body. That these men themselves are Communists I cannot believe. But one thing is sure: they have caused a very serious doubt of the entire ecumenical movement to form in the minds of millions of thoughtful Americans. This fact has real and tragic implications for the future of unified Christianity at a time when the full impact of faith is desperately needed.

I truly believe the National Council of Churches, which has done much effective work, will never fulfill its function to the highest degree as long as it permits people of this type arrogantly to misrepresent to the nation the thinking and conviction of the bulk of Protestants. I do not mean they should be denied freedom of speech, indeed, I support their right to speak, but I insist they have no right to speak for me or for millions of other Protestants who find many of their opinions repugnant.

But what about those "pronouncements" that had Jeff so riled up? And he isn't the only one either for lots of people are complaining about them. Here's the story. Some years ago the social-action zealots conceived the idea of issuing what they called "pronouncements." They probably picked up this idea from the Roman Catholic practice of issuing encyclicals. But beyond that they had evolved a new concept of Christianity as basically a social manifesto and had determined to harness the whole Christian church to their bright and eager-beaver philosophy and political viewpoint.

I know this for a fact because I was, believe it or not, one of the boys, indeed a ringleader, and am therefore well versed in just how they operate. When I was a minister in Brooklyn and later in Central New York back in the twenties, I recall how we young graduates of Boston University School of Theology would get together and plot how we could manipulate and shove left-wing resolutions through conference sessions and ultimately have them issued as "pronouncements" of enlightened thinking and give the impression they were the united opinion of the whole church.

And we knew how to do it too—don't think we didn't. The pronouncement must be couched in pious language and solemnly identified with the "will of God." It must be well interspersed with high-sounding phrases that are sacrosanct, such as "Christian ideals," "teachings of Jesus," "social passion of the prophets," "ethical insights of the Gospel" and others, all sure-fire vote collectors. Our basic social objective was buried in the heart of a maze of words, the idea being to high pressure any dissident to gulp it down like castor oil in orange juice.

Then we would plan our strategy and were we clever! We ran down the list of conference members, checking off those we could count on for sure. (Those who had gone to Boston University, Union Theological Seminary and Pacific School of Religion—they, of course, were O.K.) Then we would double-check the doubtful ones: those who were still groping in the mists of unenlightenment, who still voted Republican but who showed some signs of becoming modernized. But others we wrote off as hopeless, often with uncomplimentary references such as "skip him, he's a holy Joe," or "he's one of those dopey soul-savers," or "that Bible-toting evangelist, he's out." Few wardheeling politicians ever figured their voters better than we did ours, or with greater success.

Were we sincere? I don't know. Actually I think we were a bunch of smart alecs out to "show some of the old birds" that we really had the answers. One thing that now causes me to doubt our sincerity was the contempt we had for those who dragged their feet about going along with us. In spirit we were highly authoritarian, brooking no variance from our distinctly leftist ideas.

On getting a resolution through we were ready for the next step. Some of us were always on the committee on "public relations interpretation"—to see that the publicity was "right." We suggested headlines such as "church adopts . . ." or "church endorses . . ." The plain fact was that the church members knew little or nothing about what they read, and certainly had never "adopted" or "endorsed" any of it. Our little cell had done that; but the impression given the general public was that it was the unanimous action of the entire church.

It may be that today's agitators and wet nurses of pronouncements are more mature, though I am not too sure they are. They have had more experience, no doubt; but to an old hand with jaundiced eye the same old technique still shows through. For example, I have at hand a publicity release issued from a meeting of the General Board of the National Council of Churches held at Syracuse, New York. It is marked as coming from "Press Room—Parlor F" and reads:

"The National Council of Churches today formally approved Family Planning and Spacing in an *historic* pronouncement issued as a *Protestant consensus.*" Notice the use of the word *historic*—pronouncements are invariably *historic*. And regardless of agreement or disagreement (incidentally, in this case, agreement) I protest the use of the word *consensus*. It is consensus of the hierarchy only and is no mandate at all on the rest of us who are supposed to accept gratefully pronouncements handed down by "the best minds of our time."

One wonders why they couldn't use such phraseology as for example: "The General Board of the National Council of Churches today adopted a resolution by a 60–40 vote (that is if there are any who ever have the audacity to vote no) and respectfully asks attention to this matter by the total membership of our churches who have had no opportunity to vote on this question. This action was taken by 400 representatives not elected by the people but appointed by ecclesiastical leaders and is the expression of their opinion only. It does not commit the entire church. It is not a *consensus.*"

Perhaps the most glaring offense in the use of Protestant "consensus" was the action of the so-called Study Conference which so exasperated Jeff H_____. It seems this group was composed of some 500 delegates appointed by the hierarchy of the denominations and of the National Council of Churches and met in Cleveland, Ohio in 1959. Billed as a "Study" Conference, it issued a plea for study looking toward the recognition of Red China and its manipulators shrewdly advertised such recognition as representing the thinking of all Protestants. This action was later repudiated by an overwhelming majority (approximately 85%) in a vote taken by poll among ministers. For once the "pronouncement intriguers" went too far and were really repudiated. Perhaps Red China will ultimately be recognized, though personally I am opposed to such action; but one must ask what right had this shrewd and clever cell operating in the Cleveland meeting to seem to commit me and millions of other Protestants to an action we strongly opposed?

One thing Jeff and others complain about is that the personnel of inter-denominational groups issuing most of these pronouncements is of course very largely hand-picked by social action committees. As I've reminded those who gripe about this system, it is only human nature that they should select "birds of a feather" or like-minded people. What few others might grudgingly be admitted into conference membership are usually untutored laymen who are bewildered by glib talk and hesitate to express themselves because of lack of experience in public speaking and in the use of the jargon employed and besides, laymen have an ingrained respect for their ministers and hesitate to oppose them. So with misgivings they go along so as not to be left outside the pale and one by one drop out being fed up.

Of course, as I try to tell the irritated laymen who complain to me, Christianity has profound social implications and should make its influence felt in economic, racial or any other kind of social problem. This I firmly believe. But still I can't help agreeing that the present pronouncement obsession and method is often offensive and destructive in that it annoys and disgusts so many church members that the net result is decidedly negative. There is a better way for the church to "speak out" on social matters. It would require more time but I believe that it would achieve a more substantial result. It's this: proposed pronouncements might be sent to local churches for discussion and vote of congregations, and work their way up through the various official bodies until finally when issued by the National Council of Churches they could with more accuracy be considered the will and conviction of the churches.

But of course social action committees would hardly go for

that, since it would divest them of their jealously guarded "prerogative" in this field and too, coming up from the plain people who never have had a voice in pronouncements, might pick up too much common sense along the way to suit them.

But one thing is sure a better formula for composing committees, departments, study conferences and other gatherings would avoid the practice of packing them with the same kind of people and include a more comprehensive cross section of varying opinion. And also they should be persons who know how to present their viewpoints. The average non-leftist does not know how to articulate his views nearly as well as the more glib left-winger and so he gives up and goes along, or cynically writes the whole business off as "a bunch of lousy communists"—which, of course, is error, but an error unfortunately gaining currency.

I am fully aware that what I am saying will bring considerable abuse upon me. But so what! I've been abused by experts. I must record my conviction that a would-be-erudite, super-scholastic vocabulary-ish ethical-implication social-action type has contrived an inordinate influence upon the church. And what has been the result of their insisting upon an ethical and social emphasis above every other element in Christianity? "Protestantism," as one man said, "has sure taken a beating under these men."

The dominant faith numerically in this country and cherished for generations is, it seems now to be, steadily losing its hold upon the masses of the people. And many think it's mainly because too many leaders have tended to make of Christianity solely a social-ethical religion disregarding quite generally its supernatural character and life-changing dynamic.

As a result of the neglect of personal commitment to Christ by super-ethical implication enthusiasts, stress on individual sin languished. Laymen get the impression that the church now teaches that only society can be guilty of sin. This, of course, gives the individual an easy out from moral responsibility—and believe me individuals have taken advantage of that "out" too.

On the day the newspapers carried headlines announcing that the Presbyterian General Assembly had come out for "moderate" drinking to relieve members of being what they called "second class Christians," I had an interesting reaction from a plain church member. Maybe he was even a "first class Christian," who knows? "We have never served liquor in our home and have avoided cocktail parties thinking that there is a higher level spiritual life than our liquor centered culture. But it has been a bit hard holding those convictions since it has cut us off from some nice people who do not share our views. But now that my church is out for liquor drinking guess I'll stop by the liquor store on the way home and start lapping up the booze like everyone else." I couldn't make out whether he was hurt, let down or cynical, or maybe all three.

I said to him, "Jim, hold your own honest convictions regardless of other people's opinions and even if your church deserts you. Besides, church assemblies haven't always been right or guided by the Holy Spirit."

People are entitled to the joy and strength of the Christian life in depth. Apparently Christianity as an ethical manifesto rather than a full Gospel of conviction, re-generation and salvation allows people unsupported and unguided freely to go barging into personal hells. Furthermore it seems quite lacking in a personal crisis reference and therefore fails people in life's hard moments.

For example, a brilliant young intellectual, a desultory member of a church having an ethical-implication pastor, went to a doctor about a little pimple on his ear. A few days later the laboratory report showed Melanoma, a form of cancer. This was of course a crisis in depth in which the young man needed help, real help. His pastor proved completely ineffective. In desperation the stricken fellow turned to a man of God who not only had a vital life-changing faith but the ability to guide people to a faith-in-depth experience and help them use faith in meeting an extremity situation.

Nor was this man of God lacking in appreciation of the ethical content of the Christian religion but he had also laid hold on the power of God in a personal way. He was able to communicate God's grace to this modern intellectual in his deep crisis. The social action pastor who sincerely wanted to help had to recognize that his spiritual superficiality made him impotent in a problem of this complexity. Later after an amazing healing of the body and an even more amazing change of mind and spirit the young man said "when that thing hit me Reinhold Neibuhr and his whole intellectual philosophy couldn't have meant less to me. How grateful I am that I found a minister to whom Christ was real and who made available in my necessity the Lord's healing grace." This young man is today one of the most thorough-going and creative Christians I have ever known.

So many today are disturbed by the trend in religion. It seems that a melancholy decline of Protestantism has set in according to an article by Rev. Dr. Ralph W. Sockman in a national magazine: "During a 30-year period," he says, "the membership of five Protestant denominations in Cleveland declined more than 13 per cent. In 15 years (1940–55) some 55 churches abandoned the center of Detroit, and some major denominations lost hundreds of their city members. In the last 40 years, 44 strong Lutheran churches within two miles of the inner city have dwindled to four. Within the last century, one Protestant denomination in New York City has abandoned or merged an average of nearly one congregation a year in Manhattan and the Bronx."

Still Protestantism has had an amazing growth, especially in the burgeoning suburbia stretching for miles around great

cities out into what is now called ex-urbia or the region beyond the old and newer suburbia. Along with the migration
of big downtown shops to modern shopping centers in suburbia, many old churches from the inner city have moved to
suburbia or ex-urbia. They have followed their own crowd.

It is of course the duty and opportunity of churches to
minister to the swelling suburban population and many are
doing so admirably. But one cannot but wonder if all church
migration to the suburbs has been motivated by the noblest
objectives or whether, in some instances, it is to preserve the
social status of certain churches. Once great churches in the
inner city have declined through the years into a sort of
shabby genteelism though remnants of upper-crust families
still cling sentimentally to the old church. But would they
freely open the doors and bring into God's house and fellowship the rooming-house folk, the labor union people, the
Negroes and "foreigners" who live in the dingy old mansions
of the once socially impeccable? "Oh, no, they just aren't our
type!" and "What would dear old aunt Mabel think!" (She
would turn over in her grave.) "Oh, my, my, not those people.
Why I remember those rooming houses when the best people
in town lived there and they were all members of our dear
old church." But soon more and more of these nice old-family
people die off and then some fat wills fall due, and the next
thing you know the dear old church hightails it for suburbia
where "our kind of people now live."

A church that disregards its function as a free and open
house of God for all people of whatever economic status, national origin or color is no true church of the Lord Jesus
Christ. Any church which crassly and deliberately repels any
of God's children deserves to lose its tax exemption under law
since this financial relief by the government is related to the
true churchly function of serving all people at all times—and
we mean *all* people.

I have been pastor for thirty years of a church deep within the inner city; a church for all the people, for the whole community. It is well known that its doors are wide open for fellowship, worship and service to anyone. Economic status, social standing, color or any other factor is never raised and makes no difference at all; everyone is warmly welcomed. And we proudly number among our membership Negro Christians as well as those of other races.

If the decline of Protestantism suggested by Martin E. Martz in his book, *The New Shape of American Religion,* the magazine "Church Management" and by Russel Kirk in *Fortune* Magazine is a correct appraisal, then a serious study of the cause of such decline is indicated.

One of the strongest and most convincingly hopeful evaluation of Protestantism's current status was made by Rev. Dr. Edward L. R. Elson under the title "Is this a Post-Protestant era?" Dr. Elson, one of our greatest preachers, persuasively calls attention to the vast numbers within Protestantism, its amazing growth and development in religious education, gifts to churches exceeding three billion dollars annually, its eminent leaders and accelerated gain in membership. "Protestantism in America is neither dead or dying," he says. "It has within it the power of self-criticism which can produce self-reformation." And I like Dr. Elson's suggestion: "Let us correct what is wrong, strengthen what is weak and with zeal uphold what is right."

The chief evidence of Protestantism's being in trouble, as I see it, is the softening of its influential impact upon our culture and its lessening emphases upon the complete commitment to Jesus Christ of its adherents. Perhaps it is also primarily due to the lack of a dynamic whole Gospel preaching a de-emphasis on the Bible and conversion and a general lack of the ability to communicate with the modern masses of Americans.

In my opinion, and I say this with regret, much of the blame must be laid to those who ride the super social-action obsession, those bright, piously angry young men (older men, too) who are always asking in their stilted academic way: "Now, what are the ethical implications?" Christianity is of course an ethical code but it is much more than that; it is the power of God unto salvation and the lack of that emphasis has immeasurably subtracted from its force and appeal. The ethical social action type of preacher empties churches not because people are "conservatives and capitalists," but because the average man wants comprehensive spiritual guidance for his mind and soul. He wants a moving, life-changing message and, not getting it, the church no longer gets him.

A reason that the church seems steadily to be losing the people may be its lack of strong challenge. Its once, shall I call it, manly appeal, to face the world in God's name and to conquer it for Jesus Christ is generally missing from current preaching. The old stirring note that thrilled past generations of churchgoers is practically unknown to this generation. How many now-a-days ever get that thrill out of a sermon, a thrill that grips people so that they come out of church eyes alight, heart stirred, blood running faster. Why even this description sounds corny. But that is the way it once was in the great days of Christianity in this country. How well I remember this type of sermon hearing experience from boyhood days! And that is one reason why multitudes thronged to church; that is why religious faith penetrated the lives of our people in depth.

There was a time when great and powerful preaching fascinated and held vast congregations, and it really affected men's lives. Preachers were a rugged breed of men whose sermons were notable occasions, some of them ranking among the famous speeches of America. They had all the arts and skills of the great orators. Their evangelical zeal, sincerity and power to persuade built up and strengthened the Church to one of its highest peaks of spiritual power and influence.

And those preachers laid Christianity on the line challenging men to a big faith, giving them a world vision of Christ's kingdom, confronting them with their sins both personal and social and luring them to commitment to Christ. It was robust, powerful, man-sized preaching and robust men went for it.

How well I recall the churches of my boyhood and they were not in big cities for the most part but in middle west county seat towns. The beautiful Sunday morning sparkling and clear, the steady stream of people gathering, the hush that fell over the packed church, the sense of excitement that something great was going to happen. Then the old hymns sung by the big congregation, the moving prayer and finally the great moment when the preacher moved into his sermon catching fire until the spirit of the Lord descended upon him and upon all present. All too soon he had finished and we sat as in a spell. Christ was near, God was close by. No one who ever knew the church like this could ever forget it. It was the experience of a lifetime. This was Protestant Christianity in full flower. Out of it came many of the tough-minded optimists who made this country.

These men were succeeded by a generation that was actually taught that preaching isn't important. The "worship" service and "religious education," both important to be sure, pushed the sermon back into the status of a short, often dull and lifeless essay lacking in power, color and interest. Result: the old sermon "tasters" died off, few new ones were created to take their places and finally the drift away from the church became so marked that now the "intellectuals" in the hierarchy hopelessly admit that we are deep in the "Post-Protestant Era."

The plain fact is people are indifferent to an academic and pedantic pulpit, but they will come back and throng about a pulpit that is spiritually vital, spiritually powerful and spiritually challenging and interesting. Put the Cross at the center, summon to personal sacrifice, hold up high standards, make stern demands; in other words give real Christianity to the people and the men will be separated from the boys. That kind of church will grip and challenge the best among us. It will recover its ancient force and make a powerful impact on this messed up and pagan world. A dynamic sermon in church on Sunday morning can still be one of the most moving, stimulating, and persuasive forms of speech known to man. The modern human being can still be reached by a speech delivered with emotion, humor, and reason. There is no form of communication between human beings that has such power to move and inspire as a powerful religious address delivered by a preacher who loses himself in its delivery, pouring out his heart, his mind and his soul to his fellows.

Such a sermon combines drama, pathos, suspense, spiritual authority and indeed all the arts and skills of persuasion and it can reach modern man, no less surely than his predecessors. What a pity, what a profound pity that the people of our time should be denied the greatest form of human speech, a sermon that moves the mind and heart to an acceptance of the love of God and the redemption of Jesus Christ. This generation has little conception of the wonder and glory of Christian worship when the amazing phenomenon of a truly great sermon is at its center.

"Soul-saving" is all but a lost art in many churches. Indeed, it is a sad fact that in not a few churches not a single soul is spiritually changed in a year or in five years for that matter. In fact laymen tell me that some preachers even regard soul-saving as, shall we say, corny. I cannot believe that such an attitude could exist in evangelical Christianity—a form of faith and spiritual practice which has always sought to save the souls of individuals through the power of God and the sacrificial death and resurrection of Jesus Christ. And sadly enough along with decline in spiritual faith some of our freedoms also suffer curtailment.

Some members of the extreme ethical-implication, social action group, not all of course but some, perhaps not even many, seem strangely hostile to individual freedom of thought, speech and action. Seemingly it is inherent in their philosophy to expect and often to insist that everyone conform and not many can successfully stand against their punitive tactics. The following account in the Bangor (Maine) *Daily News* is a case in point:

> Philip *A*, a preacher who serves as pastor of the _____ Methodist Church, withdrew Friday from the right-to-work campaign after he was informed that his stand on the issue was 'out of line' with the 'Methodist view.'
>
> Knowledge of the pastor's withdrawal became public following a meeting between the pastor and his ecclesiastical superior, the Rev. Edward *X* Friday morning. Earlier in the week, both *A* and the Rev. Mr. *X* had spoken at a Legislative Labor Committee hearing. *A* supported the right-to-work bill and his district superintendent and two other Methodist ministers opposed it.
>
> After *A*'s withdrawal decision became public, the Rev. Mr. *X* attributed the young minister's previous stand to lack of experience and lack of understanding of the issue. He said *A* failed to seek the counsel of two Methodist Conference committees, one on legislative matters, before taking his stand on the matter.
>
> When asked to comment on the situation Friday, *A* would say only that 'as a minister' he had 'withdrawn formal support' of the right-to-work bill; but that 'as a private citizen' he still would 'feel free, when I am asked, to tell what I believe' about right-to-work.
>
> He did acknowledge that his decision to withdraw

from active support of the bill was 'reached between Rev. Mr. X and myself.'

Another, and of course necessarily unnamed minister, was confidentially quoted as saying "A is through." How about that! A man is "through" preaching the Gospel because he differed as a citizen and for that matter as a minister with the hierarchy of his church on a matter of public policy unrelated to dogma or creed. Protestantism founded upon the principle of "think and let think" is seemingly becoming under the authoritarian practice of ethical implication devotees, a "go along or else" degeneration of a once free spiritual movement. Of course, they probably write A off as a "queer," that being a usual definition of anyone who resists being strait-jacketed. It was reassuring to note in the same news story that the local Methodist Bishop "asserted that both the ministry and the lay membership of the Methodist Church have the right to speak their minds on social issues."

Little wonder that a once spiritually vital Protestant faith, despite huge numerical superiority and magnificent church buildings could verge perilously close to becoming an innocuous influence in American life. What else could be expected when its once sturdy belief in Jesus Christ as Lord and Saviour and the Divine Son of God was blunted; its faith in the Bible as the Revealed Word of God depreciated and the church became largely a political-social instrument; moreover one that in practice often denies the right to think and speak freely. How astonishing that the church, the body of Christ, could be exchanged for a social-political-ethical system, and one that minimizes the freedom gained by resolute men of God. People asked for the spiritual bread of life, but many of them believe they largely got the stone of social action; and so millions have grown indifferent, sometimes disgusted, and ask no more.

The need today is for a substantial spiritual leadership; for men who know how to integrate the ethical implications of the Gospel (and these are very important) with the vital life-changing individual message (which is supremely important). Indeed leaders and pastors who cannot accomplish this integration are antiquated and outmoded and scarcely competent to lead spiritually in a modern era which apparently they do not understand and which has gone by them. It is so very easy for anyone to be by-passed by time and events. How pathetic to be still scrimmaging when the ball is on down the field.

But a new day is already advanced in Protestant Christianity in the spontaneous rise of thousands of deeply spiritual groups of lay people and ministers. They have sprung up like new green shoots where old dead trees have fallen demonstrating once again that Christianity is deathless and cannot be killed by its friends any more than by its enemies. People simply must have spiritual fellowship and guidance and inspiration and so, not finding it in all too many churches, they have turned to the small intimate group. There, through spirituality in depth, many are finding God and committing their lives to Christ. So, out of the sterility and decay of Christianity in our time, emerges a new spiritual life and power. Let us therefore thank God and take courage, for all is not lost, not by a long shot. Christ still lives and sincere pastors still teach and sincere laymen still believe and practice the life changing Gospel.

Just one more word—the reader may possibly get an impression from what I have written that most pastors and preachers are as some whom I have referred to in this chapter. On the contrary, the overwhelming majority are completely dedicated men who have a sincere desire to help people, all people, in Christ's name. They are busy about their daily work of ministering to the sick, instructing youth, comforting families in sorrow, guiding the erring, and counseling the troubled. Beyond this they are trying to meet a budget, devise and carry through programs and prepare sermons designed to enlighten and inspire their people.

They have no time nor inclination to crusade in the political field. It is utterly foreign to them. They just go on, in season and out, humbly loving people in Christ's name and building up their churches. But they are alert, well educated, thoughtful men who are very much concerned about a creative identification of Christianity with the social problems of our time. Nor are they afraid to take a stand when taking a stand is indicated. And they do so with the attitude of love and humility. Their entire ministry is one of kindly and humble service to God and man. Personally I not only respect them but love them. In my opinion they are one of the finest groups of men God ever made, the faithful pastors of present day Christianity. It is indeed tragic that a few, a very few, glibly articulate super-do-gooders have been permitted to create an unhappy, and unrepresentative image of the church in the public mind.

Pastors who believe in the power of God through Jesus Christ to change lives really have the answer for our times. They know that when by an act of redemptive grace through faith in Christ, a man becomes as the New Testament says, "A new creature" if he does not also develop Christian social convictions, his commitment is less than valid.

In their thinking there is no social Gospel, no individual Gospel; there is only one indivisible Gospel. With this emphasis upon the individual and the social teachings of Jesus Christ as a unity, Christianity can become what it was surely intended to be: a spiritual religion in depth and be once again a vital force in the life of our time. And tough-minded optimists will help make it so.

WESTMAR COLLEGE LIBRARY